LEEDS UNITED

FOOTBALL CLUB

Season Review
1999-2000

MATCH CLUB GUIDE

MANAGING EDITOR: Chris Hunt
ART DIRECTOR: Darryl Tooth
ASSISTANT EDITOR: Ian Foster
SUB-EDITOR: James Bandy

LEEDS UNITED BOOK COMPILED BY: Alistair Phillips
CONTRIBUTORS: Kev Hughes, Hugh Sleight, Phil Smith,
Bev Ward, Nick Gibbs, Martin Barry, David Houghton
& the correspondents of **MATCHFACTS**.
SPECIAL THANKS TO: Rick Dorling, Ian Leach,
Tony Warner & Neil Howson at Leeds United.

First published in Great Britain in 2000 by Hayden Publishing Limited
Copyright Emap Active Ltd 2000
All rights reserved. No part of this publication may be reproduced, stored
in a retrieval system or transmitted in any form or by any means,
electronic, mechanical, photocopying, recording of otherwise, without the
prior permission of the publisher.
Colour Origination: Gildenburgh Ltd
Printed and bound in Italy by LEGO, Vicenza
ISBN 0 9533683 9 4
MATCH MAGAZINE, Bretton Court, Bretton,
Peterborough PE3 8DZ, England

www.lufc.co.uk

contents

Guide to symbols and ratings

MATCHFACTS keeps you up to date with all the vital statistics and facts about the biggest and best league in the world, the FA Carling Premiership. It comprehensively describes everything from each and every game, from player performances to the time of each and every goal, from bookings to referee's ratings and a verdict on the quality of the game. **MATCHFACTS** offers the most complete weekly football results service for your favourite team and more!

PLAYER RATINGS		MATCH RATINGS	
10 Out of this world		★★★★★ Unbelievable	
9 Outstanding		★★★★ Great game	
8 Impressive		★★★ Not bad	
7 Good		★★ Pretty dull	
6 Average		★ Terrible	
5 Below par			
4 Poor			

REFEREE: Name and rating of the match official in charge.

GAME NUMBER: Shows the type of competition played in.

Competition: **FA Carling Premiership**

Date: **Saturday April 1, 2000**

Attendance: **40,162**

Referee: **J Winter** (Stockton) 7

Game 46

MATCH RATING: ★★★   **LEAGUE POSITION:** 2nd

MATCH RATING: This mark out of five shows how good the game was.

LEAGUE POSITION: Current place in the league – also given for European games to show any place changes.

SYMBOLS: A quick way of identifying how many cards were received or goals scored during the game, explained in detail in the description below.

PLAYER NAME

SUBSTITUTION: Did the player last the whole game? If not, you can see who he was replaced by and after how long into the game it was.

TEAM: Who were Leeds playing? If you were in any doubt, it tells you right here!

LEEDS UNITED

Kewell ⚽ 🟨   ☆ 9

Goal: 44 mins; Booked: 80 mins (foul)
Subbed: 81 mins (Huckerby)

sub: Huckerby

SUB: Name of player that came on, with a rating if they played 20 minutes or more.

STAR RATING: Given to the one player from each team who made the greatest impact or contribution to their team's performance.

PLAYER RATING: An overall rating out of ten for performance, based on the impact made by the individual during the game.

THAT WAS THE YEAR THAT WAS...
1999-2000

ON MAY 14, THE FINAL MATCHDAY OF THE 1999-2000 season, Leeds United achieved something which in years to come may be cited as the first stepping stone to considerable success. A goalless draw at West Ham was not the team's most outstanding result of the season but that, combined with Liverpool's defeat against Bradford, was enough to secure third place in the Premiership and send the club into the Champions League. It was concrete evidence that Leeds, widely acclaimed as the most exciting young team in the country, had come of age.

After a season which had some exhilarating highs, it was that 0-0 stalemate which gave the Leeds manager David O'Leary his greatest thrill. "The highlights of the season for me were beating Roma at Elland Road in the UEFA Cup and hearing that final whistle at West Ham in the last game of the season, meaning we'd finished third in the league," O'Leary reflected during the close season break. "It was great to finish third. I thought we'd blown it through tiredness and I thought Liverpool had gained third position instead. Then they gave it back to us! The aim at the start of the season was to finish in the top four in the league and we really didn't expect to do as well as we did."

REWIND A FEW MONTHS BACK TO THE START OF THE 1999-2000 season. O'Leary, having been thrown in at the deep end in October 1998 by being promoted from assistant manager to replace the Tottenham-bound George Graham, had made an encouraging start to his career as a Premiership manager. He had demonstrated a great deal of confidence by introducing some promising youngsters such as Jonathan Woodgate, Alan Smith and Stephen McPhail to the side, and pulled off a transfer masterstroke by bringing David Batty back to his hometown club. Leeds, in 11th place after Graham's departure, eventually finished fourth. O'Leary had already exceeded the expectations of those who predicted the job would be too much for him, but instead of resting on his laurels he set about stamping his own authority and building his own team.

In the summer of 1999 came Danny Mills, a revelation in a relegated Charlton side, Chelsea defender Michael Duberry and, most notably of all, Michael Bridges – a precocious talent of a striker who had shown flashes of class whenever he was able to break up the partnership of Kevin Phillips and Niall Quinn at Sunderland. All three were high-profile signings recruited at a substantial cost, and football stood up and took notice – Leeds were looking good for the new season. Then came a bombshell. With the 1999-2000 season about to start, striker Jimmy-Floyd Hasselbaink threatened to go on strike if he was prevented from talking to other clubs and promptly moved to Atletico Madrid for £12 million. Hasselbaink, a virtual unknown before hitting 34 goals in 69 league games for Leeds, had been the team's cutting edge

and the focal point of the attack, and suddenly he was gone. The Leeds supporters sat down again, disappointed – maybe United wouldn't make any progress after all. Even the signing of Darren Huckerby, a striker with raw potential but not the prolific goalscoring power of Hasselbaink, failed to restore the initial optimism. It seemed like Leeds were starting the new season with a weaker team than the one which finished the previous campaign.

The opening month of the season followed this script. United began slowly, frustrated by Derby in a goalless draw at Elland Road, before Bridges exploded into life four days later at Southampton, hitting a superb hat-trick in a 3-0 win. Next came a massive test – against Manchester United at Old Trafford, and the task proved too difficult for David O'Leary's side. Despite battling well for much of the game, they couldn't make the breakthrough when chances came their way and it was the home team, with two late goals from Dwight Yorke, who ran out winners. At the final whistle there was a feeling among the fans and the watching media that Leeds were good but not that good. Not yet, anyway.

This assessment was reinforced when, after squeezing past ten-man Sunderland at Elland Road, The Whites were beaten at home by a Liverpool team without Michael Owen. With two wins against mediocre opposition, an uneventful draw and two defeats from their first five league matches, Leeds had made an average start to the campaign. There were some encouraging signs, but nothing to predict what would happen next. At the end of August, Leeds beat Tottenham at White Hart Lane and just carried on winning.

The team had suddenly clicked into place, moving up a gear and producing exciting, attacking football. Coventry were beaten in a seven-goal thriller, Newcastle went down 3-2 and Watford were seen off thanks to two fantastic strikes from Michael Bridges and Harry Kewell. The win at Vicarage Road took Leeds to the top of the table for the first time in 1999-2000 and made them the form team of the Premiership. Even the run of six successive league victories was ended in style, with Everton grabbing the last goal in a 4-4 thriller at Goodison Park. The team's success continued away from Elland Road and into Europe as they made comfortable progress in the UEFA Cup. Partizan Belgrade and Lokomotiv Moscow were no match for Leeds, who were now buzzing with confidence, sweeping past their Moscow opponents 7-2 on aggregate. United were on fire.

IT WAS THE WAY O'LEARY'S YOUNGSTERS WERE PLAYING that was winning so many admirers. More than any other team in the Premiership, The Whites were rapidly forcing themselves into the hearts of the neutral fan. Even in the club's last championship-winning season of 1991-92, the team was notable more for its graft than its craft. Under Howard Wilkinson, Leeds were disciplined and committed,

David O'Leary's side became the most exciting young team in England with their attractive, passionate football.

but not as entertaining as a team with Harry Kewell terrorising defenders en route to goal. O'Leary's predecessor George Graham was from the same mould as Wilkinson, a manager whose first move at any club is to strengthen the defensive qualities and introduce a ball-winning midfielder at the expense of a winger or creative player. David O'Leary was happy to let his young players express themselves, enjoy their football and go for goals. But there was something else about this side – just as Manchester United had captured the country's imagination by winning the title with a team of 'kids' in 1996, Leeds were trying to do the same.

Many of the youngsters had already made their mark in the 1998-99 season. Harry Kewell, Ian Harte and Lee Bowyer had been given their chance under George Graham and had established themselves as regulars by the time O'Leary took the helm. But the eloquent Irishman had no hesitation in blooding another promising graduate from the youth team, Jonathan Woodgate. The defender's progress was so rapid that within a few months of making his debut for Leeds in October 1998, he was lining up in England's defence for a crucial European Championship qualifier in Bulgaria. Woodgate wasn't the only youngster to get his chance under O'Leary. When the senior players in the side began struggling with injuries as the season went on, the United manager resisted the temptation to reach for his chequebook. Instead, he placed his faith in youth. And, to the surprise of the rest of the Premiership, Leeds just got stronger.

"We ended up using a lot of young players last season, but that was because they were the only players available," said O'Leary. "I have to say, I was very surprised by the way they played in the big games throughout the season."

WHETHER HE REALLY WAS SURPRISED BY HIS YOUNG charges or whether he was just applying his charming brand of kidology when he made that statement, no-one can be certain. What is certain is that if it was a gamble, it was a calculated one which paid off handsomely. When Alf-Inge Haaland and David Hopkin faded from the first-team and England international David Batty had his season wrecked by an Achilles injury, the gaps in midfield were quickly filled. In came Stephen McPhail, Matthew Jones and Eirik Bakke, and while Batty's experience was sorely missed, the trio of youngsters made sure the damage was minimal.

McPhail was hardly a stranger to the Elland Road faithful. The Irish midfielder had made a few appearances in the previous season and shown plenty of promise. This time, O'Leary gave him a lengthy run alongside Lee Bowyer in the centre of midfield and the Irishman gave Leeds another dimension. With a cultured left foot, McPhail's vision was a useful weapon going forward and the 21-year-old showed he could finish as well, with a brace in United's impressive away win at Chelsea in December. And being plunged into the thick of a Premiership title battle didn't do the youngster much harm. "I think the manager always had a belief in the lads he was putting in," said McPhail. "If you look through the team there's so many young players and we all grew up together, which has probably helped because we all went into the first team at more or less the same time."

"He's got faith in his players and that's the main thing. If he knows that you can do it, he'll give you a chance."
MATTHEW JONES

Matthew Jones had less experience than McPhail, but like all the other young lads at the club, he rose to the challenge when Leeds needed him. "Knowing the boss, it didn't surprise me at all," the Welshman reflected. "George Graham did a great job with the defensive side of the team, but when David O'Leary took over he just told everyone to express themselves. That's how he wanted to see the talent coming through and he wasn't afraid of playing anyone – he just chucked me in against Manchester United, Liverpool and Roma, so I was like 'cheers boss!'. It's unbelievable. He's got faith in his players and that's the main thing. If he knows that you can do it, he'll give you a chance."

The third of United's new boys really was an unknown. Eirik Bakke had been a quiet acquisition in the summer amid the big money purchases of Mills, Duberry, Huckerby and Bridges. He slipped in almost unnoticed from Sogndal in Norway and was dubbed 'one for the future' by his manager but, as is the trend at Elland Road in the O'Leary era, time passed quickly for Bakke. It wasn't long before he made the step up to the first-team squad and once he had forced his way into the starting line-up he wasn't going to move. Particularly effective in the centre of midfield but comfortable anywhere across the middle, Bakke went from strength to strength as the campaign wore on and thrived in the FA Cup in particular – the Norwegian scored four goals in only three cup ties even though Leeds tumbled out in the fifth round at Aston Villa. It was hardly a surprise to the United faithful that he received a call-up to Norway's Euro 2000 squad and made the final 22 for the competition in Holland and Belgium. Leeds had unearthed another diamond.

O'LEARY WAS TOO SHREWD TO PLACE ALL OF HIS TRUST in the club's young players, though – no matter how exciting and talented they were. He knew that as the season progressed, and as his team continued to challenge in the league and the UEFA Cup, he had to bring in reinforcements.

With the advent of the Christmas and New Year period, traditionally a stern test for teams with title aspirations, O'Leary dipped into the transfer market. His £3 million capture of Jason Wilcox was seen as a canny purchase. The Blackburn winger was one of the precious few naturally left-sided midfielders in the country and had a wealth of experience, having played in Blackburn's Premiership-winning team of 1995. Wilcox also had international pedigree, so David O'Leary had good reason to be pleased with his new signing. "I won't be afraid to buy someone for £15 million if I think he'll improve the team but if I can get people like Jason Wilcox – who I think is a bargain – I like to give it a shot that way," he said. "It just happened with Wilcox and that's the way I like to do things. All the gossip in the press is about players you're not even interested in. No-one tends to know what I'm doing and that's the way I like it."

Surprisingly, with Wilcox now on board, Leeds suffered their first real blip of form. The final fixture of 1999 at Highbury was too much for O'Leary's team as Arsenal chalked up a 2-0 victory. A few days later came an even more disappointing defeat in the Premiership, this time at the hands of a struggling Aston Villa side. Leeds became the victims of a Villa revival, going down to two goals from defender Gareth Southgate. Even one of the most memorable moments of the season, a stunning equaliser from Harry Kewell, was not enough to rescue a point.

Leeds were still top, but only just, and the advantage had been handed to Manchester United, who were in Brazil for the World Club Championship. The absence of the reigning champions was supposed to give Leeds the chance to create a good lead at the top of the table. Instead, the challenge faltered. A 2-1 win at Sunderland, with Wilcox scoring his first goal for the club and Bridges claiming the winner against his former employer, was a welcome three points, but another setback was just around the corner. After being sent crashing out of the FA Cup at Aston Villa, Leeds stumbled again in the

Harry Kewell was Leeds United's Player Of The Year in 1999-2000.

league – this time at Anfield, where Liverpool grabbed a 3-1 win with spectacular long-range strikes from Patrik Berger and Danny Murphy. Leeds were looking less like their usual bright selves and increasingly like a side that was desperately struggling to cope with a heavy fixture list.

KEWELL'S NEAT FINISH WAS ENOUGH TO BEAT SPURS AT home in February, but eight days later the title race seemed over. Manchester United, now established at the top of the Premiership, came to Elland Road for a match which Leeds had to win, or draw at the very least. They did neither. Lee Bowyer and Alan Smith both missed the kind of chances that they would have dispatched with ease earlier in the campaign, and Leeds were undone by a clinical example of goalscoring from Andy Cole. The match finished 1-0 to the treble-winners and that seemed to be the end of United's title aspirations. Even when Leeds were in pole position and cruising past teams, David O'Leary had refused to seriously consider that his team could maintain its form right until the end of the season – always insisting that the achievement was beyond his young charges this time around. But Leeds, who had occupied top spot for all but two weeks from October through to the beginning of February, had begun to believe in the dream. Not that O'Leary would admit it, of course. At least not in public.

"At the start of the season, the manager played down our chances and said, 'We know we're not going to be up there, but over the next couple of years it's going to be massive here'," revealed Michael Bridges. "But as the season went on, everyone was going on about winning the title and the boss said to the lads in the dressing room, 'Hang on a minute, we've got a hell of a chance here'." Stephen McPhail and Matthew Jones echoed Bridges' sentiments. For a young side that was brimming with confidence and goals, anything must have seemed possible and title fever had indeed infiltrated the Elland Road dressing room. "We always knew it would be a tall order but at the same time we always believed that we could do it," admitted McPhail.

"The pressure was on us and we were trying to take it off ourselves," Jones added. "The gaffer never said we couldn't win the league, he just wanted us to go out and enjoy ourselves because of the amount of young players we had in the team. He was cautious in front of the cameras, but he was like that with us, too. He urged us to give it our best shot without putting too much pressure on us. But being top of the league for so long was a tremendous experience."

Even with Manchester United looking unstoppable at the top of the league, there was still plenty to play for. O'Leary knew that a top-three finish would earn his team a place in the Champions League and that remained the primary target. Leeds were doing well in the UEFA Cup, but after comfortable wins against Partizan Belgrade and Lokomotiv Moscow, the hurdles began to get higher. They overcame Spartak Moscow in the third round on the away goals rule, then earned the prized scalp of Italian giants Roma in the fourth round. Against Slavia Prague in the quarter-finals, Leeds established a healthy 3-0 lead in the first leg with goals from Wilcox, Kewell and Bowyer. But they struggled in the return leg, relying on another strike from Kewell to win the tie 4-2 on aggregate and progress to the semi-finals of the competition.

NO FOOTBALL SUPPORTER IN THE WORLD IS LIKELY TO forget what happened before the first leg of the semi-final against Galatasaray. Suffice to say, the season was never the same for the players, management and fans of Leeds United

after the deaths of two supporters in Istanbul, and the days and weeks that followed the tragedy were dark times indeed.

The players were still expected to go about their business in a professional manner, but in the aftermath of the tragic deaths, results suffered and performances dipped. The Leeds team which played in the UEFA Cup semi-final was barely recognisable from the side which had delighted the crowd with such effervescence earlier in the season, and the outcome of the game seemed almost inevitable. But when the final whistle blew on a 4-2 defeat over two legs, there was relief that one of the saddest chapters in the history of the club had been brought to an end. "We hadn't been playing that well since around Christmas," was the honest verdict from Michael Bridges. "Then, with the Galatasaray incident things happened outside of football which obviously upset a lot of people. We were professional enough to get on with it, but that bad run was the kind of excuse that some people were looking for to knock us as a team. But before we won at Sheffield Wednesday at the end of April we'd lost something like nine games in a row."

Leeds had actually lost six games in row, but Bridges' statement reflected how long it must have seemed to a young team that was considered serious title contenders just two months before. The 3-0 victory at Sheffield Wednesday was a turning point, though, and paved the way for an improved run-in to the end of the season. Leeds beat Watford at home, then drew against Everton, with Bridges scoring his 19th Premiership goal of the season, and got a draw at West Ham – the most valuable point of the season to push The Whites above Liverpool into third place.

DESPITE THE EMOTIONAL TURMOIL OF THE FINAL TWO months, the 1999-2000 season had been a successful one for Leeds. Third position was the club's highest-ever finish in the Premier League and the highest in the top-flight since 1992. But perhaps more importantly than the points, the team took another considerable leap in development. The experienced members of the squad, such as Martyn, Radebe, Kelly and Wilcox proved how vital they were to the team's consistency, while Kewell, Bridges, Bowyer, Harte and Woodgate graduated from youngsters with potential to genuine star performers. And many other members of United's squad, including McPhail, Bakke, Jones and Smith, showed the rest of the Premiership that there is no shortage of emerging talent at Elland Road.

But perhaps the brightest talent at the club sits in the manager's chair. By the end of his first full season in charge, David O'Leary had every reason to feel satisfied with his team and with his own progress as a coach. His boys met the challenge that had been laid down for them back in August by securing a Champions League place for the following season and came close to winning the biggest prize in English football before falling away in the final months.

"When it came down to the crunch I thought we'd be out of the chase because we didn't have a big enough squad," insisted O'Leary at the end of the campaign. "I feel we could have finished higher in the league if we hadn't gone so far in the UEFA Cup. It was very unexpected that we did so well in Europe – I thought it'd be great for the team if we could reach the second or third round, although I now feel we should have got through to the final. But it was a very sad time for the team because of what happened in Turkey.

"Our aim for the new season has got to be to win a trophy. That would be good for everyone involved and for all the Leeds fans." ✪ *KEV HUGHES, assistant editor of MATCH*

"Our aim for the new season has got to be to win a trophy. That would be good for everyone involved and for all the Leeds fans." **DAVID O'LEARY**

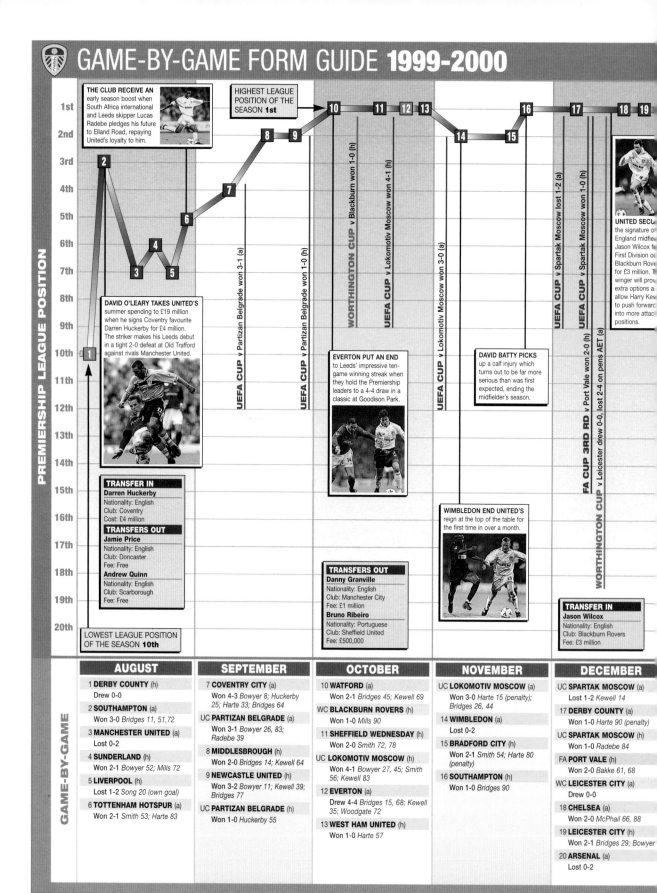

GAME-BY-GAME FORM GUIDE 1999-2000

PREMIERSHIP LEAGUE POSITION

1st 2nd 3rd 4th 5th 6th 7th 8th 9th 10th 11th 12th 13th 14th 15th 16th 17th 18th 19th 20th

THE CLUB RECEIVE AN early season boost when South Africa international and Leeds skipper Lucas Radebe pledges his future to Elland Road, repaying United's loyalty to him.

HIGHEST LEAGUE POSITION OF THE SEASON **1st**

DAVID O'LEARY TAKES UNITED'S summer spending to £19 million when he signs Coventry favourite Darren Huckerby for £4 million. The striker makes his Leeds debut in a tight 2-0 defeat at Old Trafford against rivals Manchester United.

UEFA CUP v Partizan Belgrade won 3-1 (a)

UEFA CUP v Partizan Belgrade won 1-0 (h)

WORTHINGTON CUP v Blackburn won 1-0 (h)

UEFA CUP v Lokomotiv Moscow won 4-1 (h)

UEFA CUP v Lokomotiv Moscow won 3-0 (a)

UEFA CUP v Spartak Moscow lost 1-2 (a)

UEFA CUP v Spartak Moscow won 1-0 (h)

FA CUP 3RD RD v Port Vale won 2-0 (h)

WORTHINGTON CUP v Leicester drew 0-0, lost 2-4 on pens AET (a)

UNITED SECU... the signature of ... England midfie... Jason Wilcox fr... First Division o... Blackburn Rove... for £3 million. T... winger will prov... extra options a... allow Harry Kew... to push forward... into more attack... positions.

EVERTON PUT AN END to Leeds' impressive ten-game winning streak when they hold the Premiership leaders to a 4-4 draw in a classic at Goodison Park.

DAVID BATTY PICKS up a calf injury which turns out to be far more serious than was first expected, ending the midfielder's season.

WIMBLEDON END UNITED'S reign at the top of the table for the first time in over a month.

TRANSFER IN
Darren Huckerby
Nationality: English
Club: Coventry
Cost: £4 million
TRANSFERS OUT
Jamie Price
Nationality: English
Club: Doncaster
Fee: Free
Andrew Quinn
Nationality: English
Club: Scarborough
Fee: Free

TRANSFERS OUT
Danny Granville
Nationality: English
Club: Manchester City
Fee: £1 million
Bruno Ribeiro
Nationality: Portuguese
Club: Sheffield United
Fee: £500,000

TRANSFER IN
Jason Wilcox
Nationality: English
Club: Blackburn Rovers
Fee: £3 million

LOWEST LEAGUE POSITION OF THE SEASON **10th**

GAME-BY-GAME

AUGUST
1 **DERBY COUNTY** (h)
Drew 0-0
2 **SOUTHAMPTON** (a)
Won 3-0 *Bridges 11, 51, 72*
3 **MANCHESTER UNITED** (a)
Lost 0-2
4 **SUNDERLAND** (h)
Won 2-1 *Bowyer 52; Mills 72*
5 **LIVERPOOL** (h)
Lost 1-2 *Song 20 (own goal)*
6 **TOTTENHAM HOTSPUR** (a)
Won 2-1 *Smith 53; Harte 83*

SEPTEMBER
7 **COVENTRY CITY** (a)
Won 4-3 *Bowyer 8; Huckerby 25; Harte 33; Bridges 64*
UC **PARTIZAN BELGRADE** (a)
Won 3-1 *Bowyer 26, 83; Radebe 39*
8 **MIDDLESBROUGH** (h)
Won 2-0 *Bridges 14; Kewell 64*
9 **NEWCASTLE UNITED** (h)
Won 3-2 *Bowyer 11; Kewell 39; Bridges 77*
UC **PARTIZAN BELGRADE** (h)
Won 1-0 *Huckerby 55*

OCTOBER
10 **WATFORD** (a)
Won 2-1 *Bridges 45; Kewell 69*
WC **BLACKBURN ROVERS** (h)
Won 1-0 *Mills 90*
11 **SHEFFIELD WEDNESDAY** (h)
Won 2-0 *Smith 72, 78*
UC **LOKOMOTIV MOSCOW** (h)
Won 4-1 *Bowyer 27, 45; Smith 56; Kewell 83*
12 **EVERTON** (a)
Drew 4-4 *Bridges 15, 68; Kewell 35; Woodgate 72*
13 **WEST HAM UNITED** (h)
Won 1-0 *Harte 57*

NOVEMBER
UC **LOKOMOTIV MOSCOW** (a)
Won 3-0 *Harte 15 (penalty); Bridges 26, 44*
14 **WIMBLEDON** (a)
Lost 0-2
15 **BRADFORD CITY** (h)
Won 2-1 *Smith 54; Harte 80 (penalty)*
16 **SOUTHAMPTON** (h)
Won 1-0 *Bridges 90*

DECEMBER
UC **SPARTAK MOSCOW** (a)
Lost 1-2 *Kewell 14*
17 **DERBY COUNTY** (a)
Won 1-0 *Harte 90 (penalty)*
UC **SPARTAK MOSCOW** (h)
Won 1-0 *Radebe 84*
FA **PORT VALE** (h)
Won 2-0 *Bakke 61, 68*
WC **LEICESTER CITY** (a)
Drew 0-0
18 **CHELSEA** (a)
Won 2-0 *McPhail 66, 88*
19 **LEICESTER CITY** (h)
Won 2-1 *Bridges 29; Bowyer...*
20 **ARSENAL** (a)
Lost 0-2

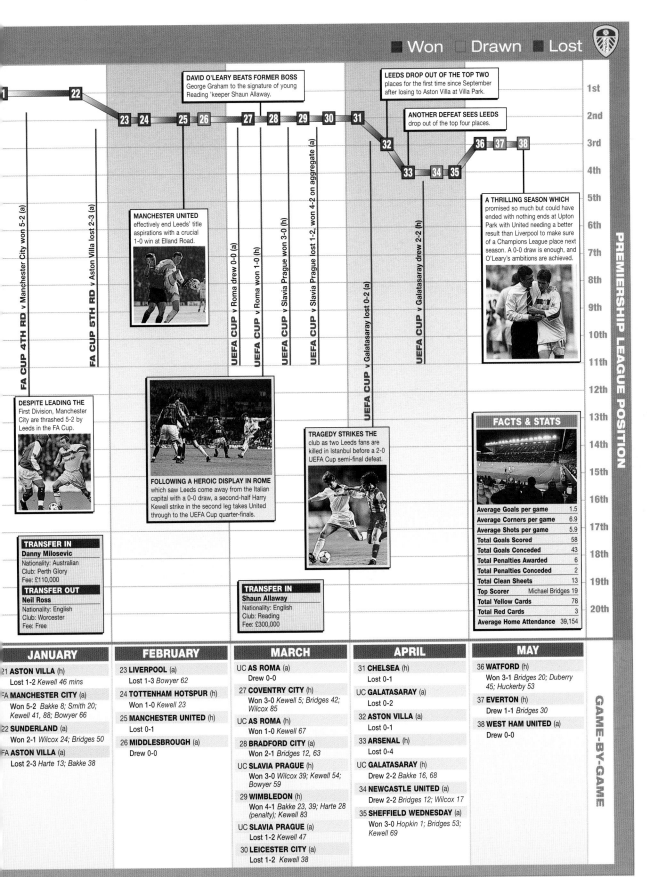

DAVID O'LEARY BEATS FORMER BOSS
George Graham to the signature of young Reading 'keeper Shaun Allaway.

LEEDS DROP OUT OF THE TOP TWO
places for the first time since September after losing to Aston Villa at Villa Park.

ANOTHER DEFEAT SEES LEEDS
drop out of the top four places.

MANCHESTER UNITED
effectively end Leeds' title aspirations with a crucial 1-0 win at Elland Road.

A THRILLING SEASON WHICH
promised so much but could have ended with nothing ends at Upton Park with United needing a better result than Liverpool to make sure of a Champions League place next season. A 0-0 draw is enough, and O'Leary's ambitions are achieved.

FA CUP 4TH RD v Manchester City won 5-2 (a)

FA CUP 5TH RD v Aston Villa lost 2-3 (a)

UEFA CUP v Roma drew 0-0 (a)

UEFA CUP v Roma won 1-0 (h)

UEFA CUP v Slavia Prague won 3-0 (h)

UEFA CUP v Slavia Prague lost 1-2, won 4-2 on aggregate (a)

UEFA CUP v Galatasaray lost 0-2 (a)

UEFA CUP v Galatasaray drew 2-2 (h)

DESPITE LEADING THE
First Division, Manchester City are thrashed 5-2 by Leeds in the FA Cup.

FOLLOWING A HEROIC DISPLAY IN ROME
which saw Leeds come away from the Italian capital with a 0-0 draw, a second-half Harry Kewell strike in the second leg takes United through to the UEFA Cup quarter-finals.

TRAGEDY STRIKES THE
club as two Leeds fans are killed in Istanbul before a 2-0 UEFA Cup semi-final defeat.

TRANSFER IN
Danny Milosevic
Nationality: Australian
Club: Perth Glory
Fee: £110,000

TRANSFER OUT
Neil Ross
Nationality: English
Club: Worcester
Fee: Free

TRANSFER IN
Shaun Allaway
Nationality: English
Club: Reading
Fee: £300,000

FACTS & STATS

Average Goals per game	1.5
Average Corners per game	6.9
Average Shots per game	5.9
Total Goals Scored	58
Total Goals Conceded	43
Total Penalties Awarded	6
Total Penalties Conceded	2
Total Clean Sheets	13
Top Scorer	Michael Bridges 19
Total Yellow Cards	78
Total Red Cards	3
Average Home Attendance	39,154

PREMIERSHIP LEAGUE POSITION

1st 2nd 3rd 4th 5th 6th 7th 8th 9th 10th 11th 12th 13th 14th 15th 16th 17th 18th 19th 20th

GAME-BY-GAME

JANUARY

21 **ASTON VILLA** (h)
Lost 1-2 Kewell 46 mins

FA **MANCHESTER CITY** (a)
Won 5-2 Bakke 8; Smith 20; Kewell 41, 88; Bowyer 66

22 **SUNDERLAND** (a)
Won 2-1 Wilcox 24; Bridges 50

FA **ASTON VILLA** (a)
Lost 2-3 Harte 13; Bakke 38

FEBRUARY

23 **LIVERPOOL** (a)
Lost 1-3 Bowyer 62

24 **TOTTENHAM HOTSPUR** (h)
Won 1-0 Kewell 23

25 **MANCHESTER UNITED** (h)
Lost 0-1

26 **MIDDLESBROUGH** (a)
Drew 0-0

MARCH

UC **AS ROMA** (a)
Drew 0-0

27 **COVENTRY CITY** (h)
Won 3-0 Kewell 5; Bridges 42; Wilcox 85

UC **AS ROMA** (h)
Won 1-0 Kewell 67

28 **BRADFORD CITY** (h)
Won 2-1 Bridges 12, 63

UC **SLAVIA PRAGUE** (h)
Won 3-0 Wilcox 39; Kewell 54; Bowyer 59

29 **WIMBLEDON** (h)
Won 4-1 Bakke 23, 39; Harte 28 (penalty); Kewell 83

UC **SLAVIA PRAGUE** (a)
Lost 1-2 Kewell 47

30 **LEICESTER CITY** (a)
Lost 1-2 Kewell 38

APRIL

31 **CHELSEA** (h)
Lost 0-1

UC **GALATASARAY** (a)
Lost 0-2

32 **ASTON VILLA** (a)
Lost 0-1

33 **ARSENAL** (h)
Lost 0-4

UC **GALATASARAY** (h)
Drew 2-2 Bakke 16, 68

34 **NEWCASTLE UNITED** (a)
Drew 2-2 Bridges 12; Wilcox 17

35 **SHEFFIELD WEDNESDAY** (a)
Won 3-0 Hopkin 1; Bridges 53; Kewell 69

MAY

36 **WATFORD** (h)
Won 3-1 Bridges 20; Duberry 45; Huckerby 53

37 **EVERTON** (h)
Drew 1-1 Bridges 30

38 **WEST HAM UNITED** (a)
Drew 0-0

AUGUST

"Everything's looking really good for the club. We had a successful pre-season and we have strengthened the squad by making some great new signings." David O'Leary

THE FIRST MONTH OF THE NEW PREMIERSHIP SEASON WAS A REAL test for David O'Leary's youngsters. They faced a schedule of six top-flight games in just 21 days – against Derby, Southampton, Manchester United, Sunderland, Liverpool and Tottenham. The opener against Derby finished in a 0-0 draw and the critics leapt on the result to say Leeds would miss the striking talents of Jimmy Floyd Hasselbaink. It didn't take long to prove the doubters wrong, though. In the very next game against Southampton, new signing Michael Bridges scored a fantastic hat-trick in a superb performance at The Dell which immediately endeared him to the Leeds faithful.

The biggest test came in the third game of the season with a trip across the Pennines to face 1998-1999 treble-winners Manchester United – an early test of Leeds' championship credentials. The team put in a battling performance at Old Trafford and possibly deserved a point, but returned home empty-handed after a 2-0 defeat. Also in August was a home game against Liverpool, a rapidly improving team under the guidance of Gerard Houllier and dark horses in the race for the championship. This was another early setback though, with The Reds winning 2-1 at Elland Road.

But Leeds emerged from August with three wins and a draw, leaving them fifth in the Premiership table at the end of the month. The Whites chalked up impressive victories against Sunderland at Elland Road and a vital 2-1 win away at Tottenham – where Alan Smith got off the mark with his first goal of the new season. In transfer news, Lee Bowyer signed a new contract that would keep him at Leeds for another four years and Lucas Radebe pledged his future to the club. After being linked with what seemed like every striker in the Premiership and beyond, David O'Leary signed Darren Huckerby from Coventry to strengthen the forward line of Michael Bridges and Alan Smith.

THE GAMES

Aug. 7 v **Derby** (h)

Aug. 11 v **Southampton** (a)

Aug. 14 v **Man. United** (a)

Aug. 21 v **Sunderland** (h)

Aug. 23 v **Liverpool** (h)

Aug. 28 v **Tottenham** (a)

TRANSFERS IN

Danny Mills

Position: **Defender**

Fee: **£4 million**

From: **Charlton Athletic**

Darren Huckerby

Position: **Striker**

Fee: **£4 million**

From: **Coventry City**

TRANSFERS OUT

Gunnar Halle

Position: **Defender**

Fee: **£200,000**

To: **Bradford City**

David Wetherall

Position: **Defender**

Fee: **£1.4 million**

To: **Bradford City**

Clyde Wijnhard

Position: **Striker**

Fee: **£750,000**

To: **Huddersfield Town**

Derek Lilley

Position: **Striker**

Fee: **£75,000**

To: **Oxford United**

MATCH facts
Matchman Of The Month

LEE BOWYER
Average Rating: 7.16

Derby's packed midfield proved hard to break down on the opening day.

FROM THE PAGES OF MATCH

At the beginning of the 1999-2000 FA Carling Premiership season, Republic Of Ireland defender **IAN HARTE** said **LEEDS UNITED** were ready to build on the successes of the previous campaign.

Is your club ready for the new season? *"Definitely. We're really looking forward to the year ahead, and we just hope we can repeat what we did last season."*

What would be a successful season? *"Some of the press are saying that we're going to be right up there with the likes of Manchester United, Arsenal and Chelsea battling for the title, but I think the boss would be more than happy if we could qualify for the Champions League."*

Who is your key player? *"Probably Lucas Radebe. He is an outstanding player, there's nothing bad I can say about him. He'll definitely be right up there for us this season."*

What about your first game against Derby? *"It will be a tough one, as they all are in the Premiership. But it's nice to play our first match at Elland Road, so hopefully we can take advantage of that and get off to the start we all want."*

What do you make of your new boys? *"I've not seen much of Eirik Bakke during our pre-season tour, but he has looked good in training. Danny Mills is an attacking right-back who likes to get forward when he can. If there's an emergency he can also fit in at centre-back, so it's useful to have Danny in the squad. Michael Bridges is very quick and when he gets a chance he'll put it in the back of the net."*

 Leeds United (0) **0**

 Derby County (0) **0**

Competition: **FA Carling Premiership**

Date: **Saturday August 7, 1999**

Attendance: **40,118**

Referee: **G Barber** (Tring) 5

Game 1

THE GAME: Leeds United fans had high hopes at the start of the new season, despite losing Jimmy Floyd Hasselbaink just days earlier. In his place, Michael Bridges, 21, and Alan Smith, 18, became the youngest ever Premiership strikeforce when they lined up against Derby. The new recruits blended in well and Harry Kewell looked dangerous from midfield, but Leeds were thwarted at every attempt as Derby packed their midfield and stifled United's attempts to play attacking football. Kewell was guilty of a miss when he was put through against Derby 'keeper Mart Poom, but the Estonian was in inspired form and the visitors were happy to leave Elland Road with a point.

MATCH RATING: ★★★ **LEAGUE POSITION:** 10th

> "You don't have to be a rocket scientist to know that we need a striker. Believe me, we have £12 million, but you don't magic them out of thin air! We have to wait to get the right one and it's going to take time." DAVID O'LEARY

LEEDS UNITED	
Martyn	6
Mills	☆ 8
Woodgate	7
Radebe	7
Harte	7
Hopkin	6
Batty ▢	7
Booked: 50 mins (foul)	
Bowyer ▢	6
Booked: 84 mins (foul)	
Kewell ▢	6
Booked: 70 mins (foul)	
Smith	5
Subbed: 55 mins (McPhail)	
Bridges	7
sub: McPhail	6

Subs not used: Haaland, Robinson, Hiden, Duberry.

DERBY COUNTY	
Poom	6
Prior	7
Carbonari	7
Sturridge	6
Subbed: 46 mins (Burton)	
Laursen	7
Delap ▢	6
Booked: 83 mins (unsporting behaviour)	
Eranio ▢	7
Booked: 45 mins (foul); Subbed: 78 mins (Borbokis)	
Powell ▢	7
Booked: 84 mins (unsporting behaviour)	
Johnson ▢	☆ 7
Booked: 58 mins (foul)	
Dorigo ▢	6
Booked: 23 mins (foul)	
Baiano	6
Subbed: 66 mins (Beck)	
sub: Burton	7
sub: Beck	6
sub: Borbokis	

Subs not used: Hoult, Schnoor.

MATCH FACTS

Shots On Target
Leeds 4-1 Derby

Shots Off Target
Leeds 5-0 Derby

Hit Woodwork
Leeds 0-0 Derby

Corners
Leeds 6-4 Derby

HOW THEY LINED UP

Martyn

Mills   Woodgate   Radebe   Harte

Hopkin   Batty   Bowyer   Kewell

Bridges   Smith

Baiano   Sturridge

Johnson   Powell   Eranio   Delap

Dorigo   Prior   Carbonari   Laursen

Poom

THIS WEEK...

IN THE NEWS

LEEDS UNITED: The Leeds team coach is attacked by Birmingham fans after a pre-season friendly... David O'Leary sells want-away star striker **Jimmy Floyd Hasselbaink** to Atletico Madrid for £12 million. The Dutch frontman says he was unhappy with the wage deal that he was offered by Leeds, which would have made him the highest paid player in the club's history... Speculation is rife over who O'Leary is lining up to replace Hasselbaink, with **Tore Andre Flo**, **Ole Gunnar Solskjaer** and **Robbie Fowler** among the names initially touted... Days later and Everton youngster **Francis Jeffers**, who's fallen out with boss Walter Smith, and Sheffield Wednesday's errant Italian, **Benito Carbone**, are added to the list of possible targets.

PREMIERSHIP: Frank Lampard and **Rio Ferdinand** agree new deals at West Ham that will keep them under contract until 2005... Southampton's veteran striker **Mark Hughes** is put in temporary charge of the Welsh national side... Arsenal sign Croatian star **Davor Suker** for £2.5 million... Tottenham boss George Graham adds to his squad by bringing Liverpool's out-of-favour **Oyvind Leonhardsen** to White Hart Lane for £2.75 million... Gary Lineker is lined up as the new presenter of the BBC's 'Match Of The Day' after Des Lynam is tempted by a big money offer from ITV.

THE FINAL SCORE!

AUGUST 7		
Arsenal	2-1	Leicester
Chelsea	4-0	Sunderland
Coventry	0-1	Southampton
Leeds	0-0	Derby
Middlesbrough	0-1	Bradford
Newcastle	0-1	Aston Villa
Sheff. Wed.	1-2	Liverpool
Watford	2-3	Wimbledon
West Ham	1-0	Tottenham

TOP OF THE PREMIERSHIP

	P	W	D	L	Pts
1. Chelsea	1	1	0	0	3
2. Wimbledon	1	1	0	0	3
3. Arsenal	1	1	0	0	3
10. Leeds	1	0	1	0	1

Southampton (0) **0**

 Leeds United (1) **3**

Game 2

Competition: **FA Carling Premiership**

Date: **Wednesday August 11, 1999**

Attendance: **15,206**

Referee: **A Wiley** (Burntwood) 7

THE GAME: Michael Bridges got off to a flying start for his new club against Southampton, and did what Jimmy Floyd Hasselbaink never achieved for Leeds by hitting a hat-trick. Saints 'keeper Paul Jones was outstanding in goal, but United were relentless coming forward. Bridges opened the scoring with a sweetly-hit volley to begin repaying the £5 million that David O'Leary paid for the striker from Sunderland. The Saints thought they had equalised on 41 minutes, but Mark Hughes saw a trademark volley rebound off a Leeds defender on the line. Bridges even had a claim for a fourth goal disallowed.

LEEDS GOALS: Bridges (11 mins): Volleyed over 'keeper Jones from 15 yards after Duberry had chested down Harte's free-kick; **Bridges** (51 mins): The Saints failed to clear a ball in their area and it fell nicely for Bridges, who couldn't miss from six yards out; **Bridges** (72 mins): Rounded off a fantastic night both personally and for his new club by completing a superb hat-trick as he popped up with an unstoppable header at the near post following Harte's precise corner.

MATCH RATING ★★★★ **LEAGUE POSITION: 3rd**

SOUTHAMPTON		LEEDS UNITED	
Jones	☆ 8	Martyn	6
Dodd	6	Harte	7
Benali ⬜	6	Radebe	8
Booked: 59 mins (foul)		Woodgate	7
Marsden	5	Hopkin	7
Subbed: 46 mins (Oakley)		*Subbed: 86 mins Jones*	
Richards	6	Bridges ⚽⚽⚽	☆ 9
Lundekvam	6	*Goals: 11, 51, 72 mins*	
Le Tissier ⬜	5	Kewell	7
Booked: 5 mins (foul)		*Subbed: 82 mins (Bakke)*	
Hughes, M ⬜	6	Bowyer ⬜	8
Booked: 70 mins (unsporting behaviour)		*Booked: 37 mins (foul)*	
Kachloul	5	Mills ⬜	7
Subbed: 66 mins (Ripley)		*Booked: 39 mins (unsporting behaviour)*	
Pahars	5	Duberry ⬜	7
Ostenstad ⬜	6	*Booked: 77 mins (foul)*	
Booked: 67 mins (foul)		Batty ⬜	7
sub: Oakley	6	*Booked: Batty 29 mins (foul)*	
sub: Ripley	6	*sub: Bakke* ⬜	
		Booked: 83 mins (foul)	
Subs not used: Almeida, Moss, Beresford.		*sub: Jones*	
		Subs not used: Haaland, Robinson, Hiden.	

MATCH FACTS
Shots On Target
Southampton 4-10 Leeds
Shots Off Target
Southampton 2-4 Leeds
Hit Woodwork
Southampton 0-0 Leeds
Corners
Southampton 6-5 Leeds

HOW THEY LINED UP

Jones

Dodd — Lundekvam — Richards — Benali

Le Tissier — Hughes, M — Marsden — Kachloul

Pahars — Ostenstad

Bridges

Kewell — Bowyer — Batty — Hopkin

Harte — Woodgate — Radebe — Duberry — Mills

Martyn

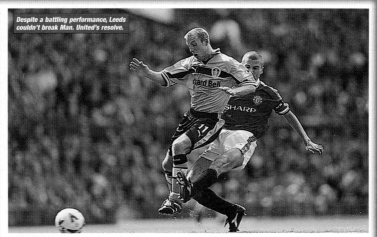

Despite a battling performance, Leeds couldn't break Man. United's resolve.

 Manchester United (0) **2**

Leeds United (0) **0**

Competition: FA Carling Premiership

Date: Saturday August 14, 1999

Attendance: 55,187

Referee: N Barry (Scunthorpe) 7

Game 3

THE GAME: Leeds put up a tough fight at Old Trafford but they couldn't match the finishing power of Dwight Yorke, who scored two late goals for Manchester United. Michael Bridges, who had scored a hat-trick in the midweek game, limped off after just 19 minutes, but Leeds battled on. The attacking football was a pleasure to watch, with both teams looking for a breakthrough. Darren Huckerby and Lee Bowyer went close, but Harry Kewell had the best chance after being put through on goal by defender Lucas Radebe. Kewell's shot agonisingly hit the post with the score at 0-0 and Manchester United went on to take the points with two clinical strikes.

MAN. UNITED GOALS: Yorke *(76 mins):* Glanced a header to the right of Martyn from eight yards out after an overlapping run by Neville on the right; **Yorke** *(80 mins):* Deadly near-post header from six yards out which went high and to the right of Martyn following Beckham's free-kick near the corner flag.

MATCH RATING ★★★ LEAGUE POSITION: 8th

> "We played well, but we'd prefer to play badly and come away with three points. That's the difference between us and them. Performance isn't the be-all and end-all. That result sickened us all, having come away with nothing — it shows we've got a bit to learn." **DAVID BATTY**

MANCHESTER UNITED

Bosnich	6
Subbed: 27 mins (van der Gouw)	
Neville, P	7
Irwin	6
Berg	6
Stam	7
Beckham	6
Keane	7
Scholes	6
Subbed: 69 mins (Butt)	
Cole ▯	6
Booked: 8 mins (not retreating ten yards for a free kick)	
Yorke ⊕ ⊕	☆ 8
Goals: 76, 80 mins; Subbed: 81 mins (Sheringham)	
Giggs ▯	6
Booked: 43 mins (foul)	
sub: van der Gouw	7
sub: Butt	6
sub: Sheringham	6

Subs not used: Curtis, Solskjaer.

LEEDS UNITED

Martyn	7
Harte	6
Subbed: 75 mins (Hiden)	
Radebe	7
Woodgate	7
Bridges	6
Subbed: 19 mins (Hopkin)	
Kewell	☆ 8
Subbed: 83 mins (Bakke)	
Bowyer	6
Huckerby	6
Mills	7
Duberry	6
Batty	6
sub: Hopkin	6
sub: Hiden	
sub: Bakke	

Subs not used: Haaland, Robinson.

MATCH FACTS

Shots On Target
Man. United 6-5 Leeds

Shots Off Target
Man. United 5-8 Leeds

Hit Woodwork
Man. United 0-1 Leeds

Corners
Man. United 5-2 Leeds

HOW THEY LINED UP

Bosnich

Neville, P Berg Stam Irwin

Beckham Scholes Keane Giggs

Yorke Cole

Bridges Huckerby

Kewell Batty Bowyer

Harte Woodgate Radebe Duberry Mills

Martyn

THIS WEEK...

MARK BOSNICH IS MANCHESTER UNITED'S FUTURE IN SAFE HANDS?

IN THE NEWS

LEEDS UNITED: Alan Smith is battling to overcome an ankle injury but the young star is eager to link up again with fellow striker **Michael Bridges**. Time is of the essence for Smith, as David O'Leary adds Coventry City's star striker **Darren Huckerby** to his forward line for £4 million... Rupert Murdoch is said to have taken personal charge of BSkyB's attempt to buy a stake in United's holding club Leeds Sporting, which could add to the Leeds manager's healthy-looking coffers... Former Leeds player **Noel Whelan** makes an apology to Coventry City fans after admitting that a return to Elland Road would be a dream come true for him.

PREMIERSHIP: Liverpool's new £8 million midfielder **Dietmar Hamann** is out for two months after picking up an injury on the opening day against Sheffield Wednesday... Aston Villa are heading the race for the exciting Wolves and Republic Of Ireland striker **Robbie Keane**... Everton's **Francis Jeffers** withdraws his transfer request at Everton after making up with Goodison manager Walter Smith... Sunderland striker **Kevin Phillips** has set himself a target of 20 goals for the season after a brace against Watford.

THE FINAL SCORE!

AUGUST 8		
Everton	1-1	Man. United

AUGUST 9		
Tottenham	3-1	Newcastle

AUGUST 10		
Derby	1-2	**Arsenal**
Sunderland	2-0	Watford
Wimbledon	2-3	**Middlesbrough**

AUGUST 11		
Aston Villa	3-0	Everton
Leicester	1-0	Coventry
Man. United	4-0	Sheff. Wed.
Southampton	0-3	**Leeds**

AUGUST 14		
Bradford	1-1	Sheff. Wed.
Derby	1-3	**Middlesbrough**
Leicester	2-2	Chelsea
Liverpool	0-1	**Watford**
Man. United	2-0	Leeds
Sunderland	0-0	Arsenal
Tottenham	3-2	Everton
Wimbledon	1-1	Coventry

TOP OF THE PREMIERSHIP

	P	W	D	L	Pts
1. Man. United	3	2	1	0	7
2. Arsenal	3	2	1	0	7
3. Aston Villa	2	2	0	0	6
8. Leeds	3	1	1	1	4

17

Leeds fought back against Sunderland to win their first home game of the season.

THE NEW RECRUIT

Name: **Michael Duberry**

Position: **Defender**

From: **Chelsea**

Signed: **July 12, 1999**

Fee: **£4.5 million**

Leeds debut: **v Southampton**

What are your first impressions of Leeds? *"It has been excellent, everything I hoped for. The whole set-up is quality and the staff have been brilliant. I have been welcomed by everyone, from the washroom ladies to the people in the canteen. Everyone has made me feel at home."*

How did David O'Leary sell the club to you? *"I think the club sold itself, to be honest. The way the club did in the Premiership last season and the direction it was obviously going in really impressed me. I thought coming to Leeds, with the young team they have, would benefit my career."*

So did you leave Chelsea to make sure you got regular first-team football? *"I thought I'd have a better chance of establishing myself in the starting line-up here. I don't want to be in and out of a team again. Watching other people play is far too frustrating for me. Phil Neville said that he'd rather play 30 games for Man. United than 50 for any other team. But Phil has played for England and has done lots of other things in his career. My choice is not to play a bit part."*

Do you think that the lack of experience in the squad will count against Leeds? *"We've got Nigel Martyn, Lucas Radebe and David Batty to give us international experience down the spine of the team. Not only that, but we've got Jonathan Woodgate, David Hopkin, Harry Kewell, Gary Kelly and Ian Harte who have all played for their country. Just because we've got a young team people assume we're inexperienced – but that isn't the case!"*

On a personal level, what do you hope for from the new season? *"A good season would be for Leeds to have the best defensive record in the Premiership and for Michael Duberry to be talked about again. I'd like to be a candidate for Young Player Of The Year or feature in the PFA Team Of The Season. People talked about me when I first came on the scene at Chelsea, but I want them to notice how much my game has developed since then."*

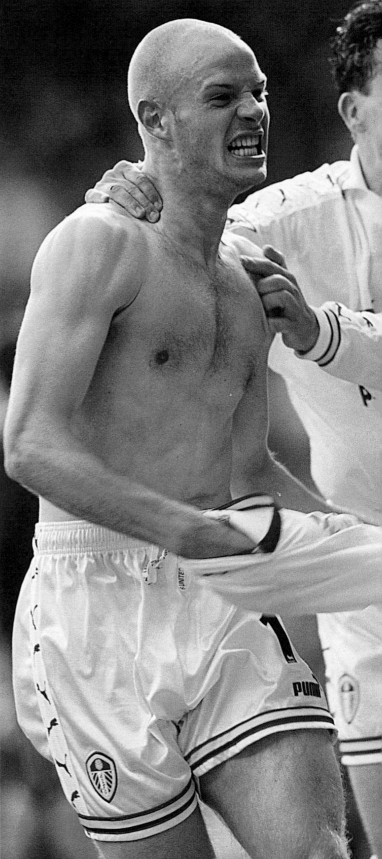

You'll never beat Ian Harte's trusty left peg, you know!

Leeds United (0) 2
Sunderland (1) 1

Competition: FA Carling Premiership

Date: Saturday August 21, 1999

Attendance: 39,064

Referee: P Alcock (Halstead) 7

Game 4

THE GAME: Despite going in a goal down at half-time, Leeds managed to hit back against Sunderland's ten men to register their first home win of the season. Peter Reid's team took the lead through a Kevin Phillips penalty in a fiercely-contested match that saw a host of bookings and the first-half dismissal of midfielder Alex Rae. However, Sunderland's goal seemed to rally United, who had two goals disallowed after Alan Smith and Michael Bridges found the net. Leeds were determined to score and it was Lee Bowyer, after an impressive performance at the heart of midfield, who got the equaliser. Danny Mills scored the winner – his first goal for the club after his transfer from Charlton – and showed exactly what it meant to him.

LEEDS GOALS: Bowyer *(52 mins):* Huckerby drifted in from the left and, as he was challenged, the ball bobbled kindly for Bowyer, who shot right-footed inside the right post from just inside the area; **Mills** *(72 mins):* Smith headed the ball down to Hopkin, whose shot deflected to Mills. The defender drove the ball through a mass of bodies from eight yards to make it 2-1.

SUNDERLAND GOAL: Phillips *(penalty 38 mins)* The Black Cats striker was bowled over by Radebe in the box and made no mistake from the spot, giving Martyn no chance.

MATCH RATING ★★★ **LEAGUE POSITION:** 5th

MATCH FACTS		
Shots On Target		
Leeds	8-3	Sunderland
Shots Off Target		
Leeds	15-6	Sunderland
Hit Woodwork		
Leeds	1-0	Sunderland
Corners		
Leeds	13-5	Sunderland

HOW THEY LINED UP

Martyn

Mills — Woodgate — Radebe — Harte

Hopkin — Batty — Bowyer — Kewell

Bridges — Huckerby

Phillips

McCann — Schwarz — Rae — Ball — Summerbee

Gray — Helmer — Butler — Makin

Sorensen

LEEDS UNITED

Martyn	7
Mills ⊕	7
Goal: 72 mins	
Harte ▭	7
Booked: 43 mins (foul)	
Radebe	7
Woodgate	7
Hopkin	6
Batty ▭	7
Booked: 41 mins (foul)	
Bowyer ⊕	☆ 8
Goal: 52 mins	
Kewell	7
Bridges	7
Subbed: 58 mins (Smith)	
Huckerby	7
sub: Smith	7

Subs not used: Kelly, McPhail, Robinson, Duberry.

SUNDERLAND

Sorensen	☆ 8
Makin	6
Helmer ▭	7
Booked: 17 mins (foul)	
Butler, P ▭	7
Booked: 6 mins (foul); Subbed: 73 mins (Quinn)	
Gray	7
Subbed: 63 mins (Holloway)	
Summerbee	7
Schwarz ▭	7
Booked: 29 mins (foul)	
Rae ▭▪	6
Booked: 39 mins (foul); Sent-off: 43 mins (second bookable offence: foul)	
Ball ▭	7
Booked: 57 mins (foul); Subbed: 90 mins (Dichio)	
McCann	6
Phillips ⊕	7
Goal: 38 mins (penalty)	
sub: Holloway	6
sub: Quinn ▭	
Booked: 88 mins (dissent)	
sub: Dichio	

Subs not used: Oster, Marriott.

Leeds United (1) 1
Liverpool (1) 2

Game 5

Competition: **FA Carling Premiership**

Date: **Monday August 23, 1999**

Attendance: **39,703**

Referee: **D Elleray** (Harrow) 6

THE GAME: Unfortunately for Leeds fans, this was the game when Gerard Houllier's new-look Liverpool side finally clicked into gear. There were few chances for either team in the first half, despite goals from Rigobert Song (putting the ball into his own net) and Titi Camara. Lucas Radebe caught the own goal curse after the break and this proved to be the decisive strike. Jamie Redknapp pulled the strings for the visitors, with England boss Kevin Keegan looking on, but it was the running of Titi Camara and Patrik Berger which caught the eye for The Reds. In a lacklustre display from United, only Lee Bowyer impressed and David O'Leary was far from happy by the end.

LEEDS GOAL: Song (own goal 20 mins): Harte's corner from the right deceived the Liverpool defence and the unfortunate Song deflected the ball into his own net, with Huckerby ready to pounce on any rebound from the inswinging cross.

LIVERPOOL GOALS: Camara (45 mins): Redknapp's quickly taken free-kick was played to Berger, who was tackled well by Radebe. But the loose ball fell straight to Camara, who sent his shot crashing into the goal via the crossbar from 18 yards; **Radebe** (own goal 54 mins): Berger broke down United's left, sending in a low cross which Radebe sliced into the corner of his own net under pressure from Fowler.

MATCH RATING ★★★ LEAGUE POSITION: 7th

LEEDS UNITED		LIVERPOOL	
Martyn	6	Westerveld	6
Mills 🟨	5	Song ⚽🟨	8
Booked: 32 mins (foul)		*Own Goal: 20 mins; Booked: 75 mins (foul)*	
Woodgate	6	Carragher	6
Radebe ⚽	7	Hyypia	6
Own Goal: 54 mins		Matteo	7
Harte	6	Thompson	7
Hopkin	5	Gerrard	6
Subbed: 68 mins (Bakke)		Redknapp	8
Batty	6	Camara ⚽🟨	8
Bowyer 🟨	☆ 8	*Goal: 45 mins; Booked: 80 mins (foul)*	
Booked: 17 mins (foul)		Berger	☆ 9
Kewell	5	Fowler	6
Huckerby	5	*Subs not used: Staunton, Meijer, Friedel, Murphy, Traore.*	
Bridges	5		
Subbed: 57 mins (Smith)			
sub: Bakke	6		
sub: Smith	5		
Subs not used: Kelly, Robinson, Duberry.			

MATCH FACTS

Shots On Target
Leeds 3-7 Liverpool

Shots Off Target
Leeds 5-3 Liverpool

Hit Woodwork
Leeds 0-0 Liverpool

Corners
Leeds 4-3 Liverpool

HOW THEY LINED UP

Martyn

Mills Woodgate Radebe Harte

Bowyer Batty Hopkin Kewell

Bridges Huckerby

Fowler Camara

Berger Redknapp Gerrard Thompson

Matteo Carragher Hyypia Song

Westerveld

Spurs tried to keep everything covered, but United's Ian Harte had other ideas.

Tottenham Hotspur (1) 1
Leeds United (0) 2

Competition: **FA Carling Premiership**

Date: **Saturday August 28, 1999**

Attendance: **36,012**

Referee: **M Reed** (Birmingham) 7

Game 6

THE GAME: Tottenham's Les Ferdinand was carried off after just two minutes of this highly-charged game, but the striker returned to cause havoc in United's defence in the first half. The first 45 minutes were played at a frantic pace and in an end-to-end battle, Leeds 'keeper Nigel Martyn made a truly outstanding save from a Steffen Iversen header following Tim Sherwood's cross. After going 1-0 down before the break, the troublesome Ferdinand was replaced at half-time and Leeds took full advantage. After coming back from a goal down to lead 2-1, the United supporters started to taunt ex-manager George Graham. The result was marred by the late dismissal of Alan Smith, who was sent-off for two bookable offences, but it was too late for Spurs to take advantage of the ten men.

TOTTENHAM GOAL: Sherwood *(36 mins)*: A long throw-in from German international Freund found Iversen, who held the pass up well and knocked it back for Sherwood to power the ball into the bottom left-hand corner of the goal.

LEEDS GOALS: Smith *(53 mins)*: Turned and shot from the edge of the penalty area into the bottom left-hand corner of Walker's goal; Harte *(83 mins)*: Crashed a direct free-kick from the edge of the penalty box into the Tottenham net.

MATCH RATING ★★★ LEAGUE POSITION: 5th

MATCH FACTS	
Shots On Target	
Tottenham 6-4 Leeds	
Shots Off Target	
Tottenham 8-6 Leeds	
Hit Woodwork	
Tottenham 0-0 Leeds	
Corners	
Tottenham 6-5 Leeds	

HOW THEY LINED UP

Walker
Carr — Perry — Young — Taricco
Leonhardsen — Freund — Sherwood — Ginola
Iversen — Ferdinand

Smith — Bridges
Kewell — Batty — Bowyer
Harte — Woodgate — Radebe — Duberry — Mills
Martyn

TOTTENHAM HOTSPUR

Walker	7
Carr	6
Perry	7
Young	6
Taricco	6
Booked: 26 mins (foul)	
Leonhardsen	6
Sherwood	★ 8
Goal: 36 mins	
Freund	7
Booked: 65 mins (foul)	
Ginola	7
Iversen	7
Ferdinand	7
Subbed: 46 mins (Dominguez)	
sub: Dominguez	7
Subbed: 84 mins (Nielsen)	

Subs not used: Baardsen, Fox, King.

LEEDS UNITED

Martyn	★ 8
Duberry	7
Booked: 54 mins (foul)	
Radebe	7
Booked: 66 mins (foul)	
Woodgate	6
Subbed: 46 mins (Hopkin)	
Mills	7
Subbed: 65 mins (Kelly)	
Batty	6
Bowyer	7
Booked: 23 mins (foul)	
Kewell	7
Harte	7
Goal: 83 mins	
Smith	7
Goal: 53 mins; Booked: 62 mins (foul); Sent-off: 87 mins (second bookable offence: violent conduct)	
Bridges	6
Booked: 35 mins (foul); Subbed: 46 mins (Huckerby)	
sub: Hopkin	6
sub: Huckerby	6
sub: Kelly	6

Subs not used: Robinson, Haaland.

SEPTEMBER

> "The young players here are good enough – don't worry about that. That extra bit of experience will come in time and the future looks good for the club." David Batty

SEPTEMBER BROUGHT NEW CHALLENGES TO ELLAND ROAD, MOST notably the start of Leeds' UEFA Cup campaign. Two legs against Partizan Belgrade of Yugoslavia at the end of the month tested what the youngsters were made of and called on the experience of Nigel Martyn, Lucas Radebe and David Batty. The entire team passed this first European test in emphatic fashion with a convincing 3-1 away win in the first leg of the tie to make the return leg at Elland Road a formality for David O'Leary's improving side.

The month began with a trip to Coventry in the Premiership, where there were plenty of old scores to be settled. The manager at Highfield Road, Gordon Strachan, and captain Gary McAllister both won the championship with Leeds as players, while striker Noel Whelan was also an Elland Road regular at one time. The liveliest reception of the day, however, was reserved by the Coventry faithful for Darren Huckerby, who returned to Highfield Road just weeks after moving to Leeds in a £4 million deal.

The Whites were victorious, winning 4-3 in an epic contest with Huckerby scoring against his old club. From that point onwards, things just got better as the month went on. After disposing of the potentially dangerous Partizan Belgrade, Leeds gained maximum points in the three league games against Coventry, Middlesbrough and Newcastle, and the goals flowed for O'Leary's new-look attack to lift the team into second place in the Premiership. With five straight wins in September, Leeds took their record to six consecutive victories, and with the October timetable looking appetising, the team was looking forward to every single game with eager anticipation.

Things were looking good financially, too. A new kit deal with sportswear giants Nike meant a substantial amount of new investment for the club and proved, if anyone was in any doubt, that Leeds had become a major player.

MATCH *facts*

Matchman Of The Month

HARRY KEWELL
Average Rating: 7.33

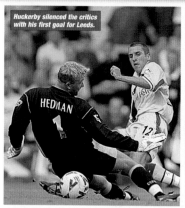

Huckerby silenced the critics with his first goal for Leeds.

Coventry City (2) 3
Leeds United (3) 4

Competition: FA Carling Premiership

Date: **Saturday September 11, 1999**

Attendance: **21,532**

Referee: **S Dunn** (Bristol) 5

Game 7

THE GAME: In this seven-goal thriller at Highfield Road, both sides were ruthlessly exposed for the frailty of their defences. Coventry got off to a dream start but allowed Leeds to get back into the game. The Sky Blues played some entertaining football, with Youssef Chippo catching the eye in midfield, but David O'Leary's team fought back. Darren Huckerby scored his first goal for Leeds against his former club to make it 2-2, before Ian Harte's penalty put United ahead for the first time in the match – and there were still only 33 minutes on the clock. Michael Bridges capped another fine performance with the winning goal after Coventry had pulled the score back to 3-3.

COVENTRY GOALS: McAllister (penalty 2 mins): Hopkin handled McAllister's shot and referee Dunn pointed to the spot. McAllister calmly tucked away the resulting penalty-kick; **Aloisi** (17 mins): Radebe blocked a shot and the ball ran loose to McAllister, who put over a cross which Aloisi glanced home from close range; **Chippo** (54 mins): Scored with a rising shot into the roof of the net to claim the best goal of the game.

LEEDS GOALS: Bowyer (8 mins): The midfielder needed two attempts before scoring after his first shot hit Hedman, but he made no mistake from the rebound; **Huckerby** (25 mins): The former Coventry frontman picked up Batty's cross and raced through to beat the 'keeper and make it 2-2; **Harte** (penalty 33 mins): Batty was brought down in the penalty area by Hedman and left Harte to convert the spot-kick with a left-footed drive; **Bridges** (64 mins): A finely-weighted pass from Kewell found his team-mate Bridges, who got the winner from close range.

MATCH RATING ★★★ LEAGUE POSITION: 4th

MATCH FACTS

Shots On Target	
Coventry 7-6 Leeds	
Shots Off Target	
Coventry 5-7 Leeds	
Hit Woodwork	
Coventry 0-1 Leeds	
Corners	
Coventry 8-10 Leeds	

COVENTRY CITY

Player		Rating
Hedman		5
Edworthy		6
Williams		7
Shaw		6
McAllister ⚽ ▭		6
Goal: 2 mins; Booked: 71 mins (dissent)		
Hadji ▭		6
Booked: 11 mins (foul)		
Froggatt		5
Subbed: 76 mins (McSheffrey)		
Chippo ⚽	☆	8
Goal: 54 mins		
Quinn ▭		6
Booked: 63 mins (foul); Subbed: 76 mins (Strachan)		
Keane		6
Aloisi ⚽		6
Goal: 17 mins; Subbed: 56 mins (Hall)		
sub: Hall		6
sub: McSheffrey		
sub: Strachan		
Subs not used: Konjic, Nuzzo.		

LEEDS UNITED

Player		Rating
Martyn		6
Harte ⚽		6
Goal: 33 mins (penalty); Subbed: 62 mins (Kelly)		
Radebe	☆	8
Mills ▭		6
Booked: 73 mins (foul)		
Duberry		6
Subbed: 65 mins (Woodgate)		
Hopkin ▭		6
Booked: 70 mins (foul)		
Kewell		7
Bowyer ⚽		6
Goal: 8 mins		
Batty		6
Huckerby ⚽		7
Goal: 25 mins		
Bridges ⚽		6
Goal: 64 mins		
sub: Kelly		6
sub: Woodgate		6
Subs not used: Haaland, Robinson, Jones.		

HOW THEY LINED UP

Hedman

Edworthy Shaw Williams Froggatt

Hadji McAllister Chippo Quinn

Keane Aloisi

Bridges Huckerby

Kewell Bowyer Batty Hopkin

Harte Radebe Duberry Mills

Martyn

DESIGNER MENSWEAR

IN THE NEWS

LEEDS UNITED: David O'Leary has been given all of the £13.8 million that BSkyB has invested into the club for its 9.9 per cent share of Leeds Sporting. When this is added to the £12 million received for the sale of Jimmy Floyd Hasselbaink, plus money made available for new signings, the Leeds boss has a substantial amount of money to spend on improving his squad… Hasselbaink is reportedly causing unrest at his new club, Atletico Madrid, by demanding that he is allowed to take all the free-kicks within range of goal…. **David Robertson** has turned down the offer of a loan move to nearby Barnsley after a trial at the club.

PREMIERSHIP: Twenty seven players and staff at Leicester City are charged by the Football Association in connection with an investigation into black market ticket sales at the Worthington Cup Final last season against Spurs… Tony Blair intervenes to grant **Juninho** a work permit, which will allow the Brazilian star to return to Middlesbrough on loan until the end of June… Young Manchester United defender **Ronnie Wallwork** has been hit with a lifetime ban by the Belgian FA after he attacked a referee while playing on loan for Belgian league side Royal Antwerp.

THE FINAL SCORE!

SEPTEMBER 11		
Arsenal	3-1	Aston Villa
Chelsea	1-0	Newcastle
Coventry	3-4	**Leeds**
Liverpool	2-3	**Man. United**
Middlesbrough	3-2	Southampton
Sheff. Wed.	0-2	**Everton**
Sunderland	2-0	Leicester
West Ham	1-0	Watford
Wimbledon	2-2	Derby

TOP OF THE PREMIERSHIP					
	P	W	D	L	Pts
1. Man. United	7	6	1	0	19
2. Chelsea	5	4	1	0	13
3. West Ham	5	4	1	0	13
4. Leeds	7	4	1	2	13

It was the Partizan players who had headaches at the end of 90 minutes.

FROM THE PAGES OF MATCH

LEEDS qualified for the UEFA Cup last season after finishing fourth in the 1998-99 Premier League. New striker **DARREN HUCKERBY** was looking forward to the new challenge that lay ahead.

How do you see the first game going? *"We've had to wait a while to find out where the away game is going to be played, because Partizan are from Yugoslavia and obviously there has been a lot of violence in that area. Now we've been told we're going to have to play in Holland. When we do play, the main aim is to get an away goal and then build on that when we get back to Elland Road."*

How far can you go in Europe this year? *"I don't know, I haven't thought about it to be honest. We're just looking as far as the first game and if we can get past that round, we'll have to wait to see who we get drawn against next. You can never tell because the luck of the draw is vital."*

Where does the UEFA Cup fall in your priorities? *"All the competitions are important to us. I think the Premier League is the most important, but then you've also got the three cup competitions and they all carry their own worth. I'd say the UEFA Cup is second on our list of priorities."*

What will be your biggest asset in this competition? *"I think the youthfulness of the squad, with the excitement of getting into Europe this season, will make an enormous difference for us. We've got that youthful enthusiasm and then we've also got plenty of experience with international players like Lucas Radebe and David Batty in the side. That combination should stand us in good stead for Europe."*

Leeds tried not to get carried away after a comfortable win.

IN THE NEWS

LEEDS UNITED: Nigel Martyn is on top form for England in the Euro 2000 qualifiers against Poland and Luxembourg, keeping two clean sheets... **David Batty** responds to taunts from the opposing fans after being sent-off for England against Poland... David O'Leary refuses to be drawn into an argument in the build-up to the big European clash with Partizan Belgrade. Partizan manager Miodrag Jovic accuses Leeds of running scared after the club asked to play the first leg of the tie at a neutral venue because of the politically unstable situation in Belgrade.

PREMIERSHIP: Martin O'Neill's position as manager of Leicester City is uncertain as the power struggle in the club's boardroom continues to drag on. O'Neill's future depends on whether his allies, chairman John Elsom and Plc chief executive Sir Rodney Walker, emerge victorious from the battle... Only 250,000 people throughout Britain tune in to watch Manchester United and Arsenal open their Champions League campaigns, which are screened on ONdigital... Watford manager Graham Taylor smashes the club transfer record to sign striker **Nordin Wooter** from Spanish side Real Zaragoza for £975,000.

THE FINAL SCORE!

SEPTEMBER 12		
Bradford	1-1	Tottenham

SEPTEMBER 18		
Aston Villa	1-0	Bradford
Derby	0-5	**Sunderland**
Leicester	2-2	Liverpool
Man. United	1-1	Wimbledon
Southampton	0-1	**Arsenal**
Watford	1-0	Chelsea

Partizan Belgrade (1) 1
Leeds United (2) 3

Competition: UEFA Cup 1st Rd, 1st Leg

Game 8

Date: Tuesday September 14, 1999

Attendance: 4,000

Referee: H Fandel (Germany) 6

THE GAME: David O'Leary was delighted with his young team's performance in Holland as they controlled their UEFA Cup first round, first leg tie against Partizan Belgrade. Despite going a goal down in the 21st minute, Leeds battled hard to get back into the game, with Lee Bowyer equalising with a great left-foot effort. At 1-1, Nigel Martyn saved Rasovic's penalty after Radebe pulled down Kezmann. The defender made up for his error by putting Leeds in front before the break and United were dominant in the second half. Bowyer sealed the victory with a late strike to wrap up an excellent team performance and give Leeds a priceless away win.

PARTIZAN GOAL: Tomic (21 mins): Martyn could only parry Kezmann's shot to Tomic, who slotted home from eight yards.

LEEDS GOALS: Bowyer (26 mins): A weak punch from the 'keeper fell to Bowyer, who brought the ball down and struck a terrific half-volley into the net; **Radebe** (39 mins): Harte floated in a free-kick from the right, and although the Leeds skipper stumbled to the floor, he still managed to acrobatically hook the ball into the top left-hand corner of the net; **Bowyer** (83 mins): Spun on the edge of the box to get the ball onto his left. Damjanac made a dreadful fumble in Partizan's goal and could only watch as the ball spun behind him and into the net.

MATCH RATING ★★★★ LEAGUE POSITION: 5th

> "There are similarities between this Leeds team and the great side of all those years ago. We had the same togetherness that these lads have now." LEEDS LEGEND PETER LORIMER

PARTIZAN BELGRADE

Damjanac	4
Savic	6
Rasovic	6
Stanojevic	6
Krstajic	6
Trobok	7
Ivic	6
Subbed: 89 mins (Stojakovic)	
Ilic	7
Subbed: 82 mins (Gerasimovski)	
Tomic ⚽ 🟨	7
Goal: 21 mins; Booked: 45 mins (foul)	
Ilijev	6
Subbed: 70 mins (Pekovic)	
Kezmann	☆ 7
sub: Pekovic	6
sub: Stojakovic	
sub: Gerasimovski	

Subs not used: *Duljaj, Miskovic, Vukovic, Pantic.*

LEEDS UNITED

Martyn	7
Mills	7
Woodgate	7
Radebe ⚽	7
Goal: 39 mins	
Harte	7
Kelly	7
Bowyer ⚽ 🟨 ⚽	☆ 8
Goals: 26, 83 mins; Booked: 31 mins (foul)	
Batty	7
Hopkin	7
Kewell	7
Bridges 🟨	7
Booked: 43 mins (unsporting behaviour); Subbed: 70 mins (Smith)	
sub: Smith	6

Subs not used: *Haaland, Huckerby, Robinson, Hay, Bakke, Hiden.*

MATCH FACTS

Shots On Target
Partizan 4-7 Leeds

Shots Off Target
Partizan 5-7 Leeds

Hit Woodwork
Partizan 0-0 Leeds

Corners
Partizan 1-8 Leeds

HOW THEY LINED UP

Damjanac

Rasovic Krstajic Ivic Savic

Ilic Stanojevic Trobok Kezmann

Tomic Ilijev

Kewell Bridges

Hopkin Batty Bowyer Kelly

Harte Woodgate Radebe Mills

Martyn

TOP OF THE PREMIERSHIP					
	P	W	D	L	Pts
1. Man. United	8	6	2	0	20
2. Arsenal	8	5	1	2	16
3. Aston Villa	8	5	1	2	16
5. Leeds	7	4	1	2	13

The job all defenders dread… having to mark Harry Kewell.

Leeds came through a hard-fought game with Newcastle to win 3-2.

Leeds United	(1)	**2**
Middlesbrough	(0)	**0**

Competition: FA Carling Premiership

Date: Sunday September 19, 1999

Attendance: 34,122

Referee: D Gallagher (Banbury) 6

Game 9

THE GAME: Harry Kewell scored his first goal of the season as David O'Leary's side took maximum points from a testing game against Middlesbrough at Elland Road. The Wizard of Oz, whose last goal for Leeds was way back in March 1999, ended his goal drought with a fantastic 30-yard effort in the 64th minute after Darren Huckerby's effort had rebounded off Boro goalkeeper Mark Schwarzer. Leeds played some neat passing football in the first half and went ahead as early as the 14th minute, with Michael Bridges scoring his fifth goal of the season. Paul Ince did his best to spark a Middlesbrough revival as he led by example in midfield, but Kewell's strike in the second half effectively killed off the game and made sure Leeds took the three points.

LEEDS GOALS: Bridges (14 mins): Scored a deflected volley off defender Vickers from a good right-wing cross supplied by Smith; **Kewell** (64 mins): Huckerby's first attempt rebounded off Boro 'keeper Schwarzer, leaving Kewell to accurately fire into the empty net from 30 yards out.

MATCH RATING ★★★ LEAGUE POSITION: 2nd

> "More goals will come. I've got a bet with Harry and he has a target to reach to make me pay out. If I lose this one I might not be going on holiday." DAVID O'LEARY

LEEDS UNITED

Martyn	7
Mills	6
Radebe	7
Woodgate	7
Harte	6
Hopkin	6
Subbed: 46 mins (Kelly)	
Batty	7
Bowyer 🟨	7
Booked: 59 mins (foul).	
Kewell ⊕	☆ 8
Goal: 64 mins	
Bridges ⊕	7
Goal: 14 mins; Subbed: 53 mins (Huckerby)	
Smith	6
sub: Kelly	6
sub: Huckerby	6

Subs not used: Haaland, Robinson, Bakke

MIDDLESBROUGH

Schwarzer	6
Festa 🟨	6
Booked: 74 mins (handball)	
Vickers	6
Pallister 🟨	6
Booked: 69 mins (foul)	
Cooper	7
Ziege 🟨	6
Booked: 77 mins (foul)	
Mustoe	7
Ince 🟨	☆ 8
Booked: 88 mins (foul)	
O'Neill	7
Deane	7
Armstrong	6
Subbed: 72 mins (Ricard)	
sub: Ricard	

Subs not used: Fleming, Beresford, Maddison, Gavin.

Leeds United	(2)	**3**
Newcastle United	(1)	**2**

Competition: FA Carling Premiership

Date: Saturday September 25, 1999

Attendance: 40,192

Referee: B Knight (Orpington) 5

Game 10

THE GAME: Leeds made it five wins on the trot and England manager Kevin Keegan left Elland Road a contented man after watching Alan Shearer score twice. Michael Bridges, who was brought up in Newcastle, missed a host of chances but made amends by tucking away the winner 13 minutes from the end. Young stars Lee Bowyer and Harry Kewell had put Leeds two goals in front, but Newcastle skipper Shearer made them work hard for the points in front of Elland Road's biggest crowd of the season. The 3-2 win put David O'Leary's side into second place in the Premiership behind leaders Manchester United.

LEEDS GOALS: Bowyer (11 mins): Bakke played a testing through-ball to Bowyer, who shot right-footed over Harper from inside the box; **Kewell** (39 mins): Batty sent over a high cross from right midfield and Kewell stormed in to head home emphatically after the ball had bounced into his path; **Bridges** (77 mins): Bowyer's pass from midfield picked out substitute Huckerby, whose cross from the left was fired into the bottom right-hand corner of the net by the in-form Bridges.

NEWCASTLE GOALS: Shearer (42 mins): Solano planted a free-kick into the goalmouth and Shearer beat Radebe to head home; **Shearer** (53 mins): Domi's throughball found Dyer inside the box on the left. The midfielder squared perfectly for Shearer to rifle a stunning eight-yard shot past Martyn.

MATCH RATING ★★★ LEAGUE POSITION: 2nd

> "With Alan Shearer you know you've been in a game. He scores goals, he can shoot, he can head, he's quick and he can hold the ball up. You can hardly get near him, you have to position yourself off him." JONATHAN WOODGATE

MATCH FACTS

Shots On Target
Leeds 9-7 Middlesbrough

Shots Off Target
Leeds 11-8 Middlesbrough

Hit Woodwork
Leeds 0-0 Middlesbrough

Corners
Leeds 8-5 Middlesbrough

HOW THEY LINED UP

Martyn

Mills · Radebe · Woodgate · Harte

Hopkin · Batty · Bowyer · Kewell

Bridges · Smith

Deane · Armstrong

Ziege · O'Neill · Ince · Mustoe

Festa · Vickers · Pallister · Cooper

Schwarzer

Leeds United (0) 1
Partizan Belgrade (0) 0

Leeds win 4-1 on aggregate.

Competition: UEFA Cup 1st Rd, 2nd Leg

Date: Thursday September 30, 1999

Attendance: 39,806

Game 11

Referee: F Stuchlik (Austria) 6

THE GAME: Leeds strolled through to the UEFA Cup second round without breaking sweat. Armed with their 3-1 advantage from the first leg, United comfortably guarded their lead and Darren Huckerby scored the winner with his first ever goal in European competition. Leeds stretched their winning streak to six straight matches, their best run for 26 years, but Partizan – without five of the players who had played in the first leg – provided poor opposition. The 1-0 scoreline did not reflect United's domination of the match, with Lee Bowyer shooting over the bar from six yards out, and Hopkin and Kewell also missing chances, but it was a vital win nevertheless.

LEEDS GOALS: Huckerby *(55 mins):* Received the ball from Kewell inside the box and easily rounded the 'keeper before slotting the ball into the Partizan net from a narrow angle.

MATCH RATING ★★ LEAGUE POSITION: 2nd

> *"It's a learning curve for us. It's an adventure for the players and I hope we can do well and get through a few rounds."* DAVID O'LEARY

THIS WEEK...

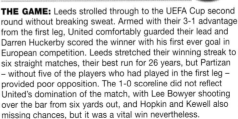

MICHAEL OWEN

IN THE NEWS

LEEDS UNITED: David Batty is handed a two game international ban after being sent-off during the European Championship qualifier with Poland… Republic Of Ireland star **Stephen McPhail** could be out of action for a month with an ankle injury… England Under-21 midfielder **Lee Bowyer** is suffering with a hamstring injury but he will continue to play despite the great discomfort he is feeling between games… Leeds seal a brand new four-year kit deal with sportswear giants Nike.

PREMIERSHIP: The former Nottingham Forest manager Brian Clough expresses his displeasure at Manchester United pulling out of the FA Cup to play in Brazil in January and says he hopes they all get diarrhoea… Troubled Aston Villa striker **Stan Collymore** is linked with a move to Turkey, with both Besiktas and Galatasaray interested… Chelsea are said to be in the hunt for **Luis Enrique** of Barcelona… Southampton agree to sell The Dell to Barrett Homes for £5 million. The money will be used to help fund a long-awaited move to a 32,000-seater stadium.

THE FINAL SCORE!

SEPTEMBER 19

Everton	1-0	West Ham
Leeds	2-0	Middlesbrough
Newcastle	8-0	Sheff. Wed.
Tottenham	3-2	Coventry

SEPTEMBER 25

Arsenal	1-0	Watford
Coventry	1-0	West Ham
Derby	0-1	**Bradford**
Leeds	3-2	Newcastle
Leicester	3-1	Aston Villa
Man. United	3-3	Southampton
Middlesbrough	0-1	**Chelsea**
Sunderland	1-0	Sheff. Wed.

SEPTEMBER 26

Wimbledon	1-1	Tottenham

SEPTEMBER 27

Liverpool	0-1	**Everton**

TOP OF THE PREMIERSHIP

	P	W	D	L	Pts
1. Man. United	9	6	3	0	21
2. Leeds	9	6	1	2	19
3. Arsenal	9	6	1	2	19
4. Sunderland	9	5	2	2	17

LEEDS UNITED

Martyn ▢	6
Booked: 40 mins (foul)	
Kelly ▢	7
Booked: 79 mins (foul)	
Radebe ▢	5
Booked: 46 mins (foul)	
Woodgate	6
Harte	6
Bakke	7
Subbed: 78 mins (Haaland)	
Batty ▢	7
Booked: 83 mins (foul)	
Bowyer ⊕ ☆	8
Goal: 11 mins	
Kewell ⊕	7
Goal: 39 mins	
Smith ▢	6
Booked: 60 mins (foul); Subbed: 73 mins (Huckerby)	
Bridges ⊕	6
Goal: 77 mins	
sub: *Huckerby*	
sub: *Haaland*	
Subs not used: Mills, Jones, Robinson.	

NEWCASTLE UNITED

Harper	7
Barton	7
Marcelino ▢	6
Booked: 31 mins (foul)	
Goma	6
Domi ▢	6
Booked: 6 mins (foul)	
Solano	6
McClen	5
Subbed: 73 mins (Charvet)	
Speed ▢	6
Booked: 75 mins (foul)	
Dyer ☆	8
Ketsbaia	6
Shearer ⊕ ⊕	7
Goals: 42, 53 mins	
sub: *Charvet*	
Subs not used: Glass, Hughes, Robinson, Wright.	

LEEDS UNITED

Martyn	7
Kelly	6
Woodgate	7
Radebe	7
Harte	7
Hopkin	7
Subbed: 81 mins (Bakke)	
Batty ☆	8
Bowyer ▢	7
Booked: 49 mins (foul)	
Kewell	7
Subbed: 85 mins (Jones)	
Bridges	6
Subbed: 68 mins (Smith)	
Huckerby ⊕	7
Goal: 55 mins	
sub: *Smith*	7
sub: *Bakke*	
sub: *Jones*	
Subs not used: Haaland, Mills, Hay, Robinson.	

PARTIZAN BELGRADE

Damjanac	6
Savic	6
Sabo	6
Gerasimovski	7
Stanojevic	6
Trobok	7
Subbed: 67 mins (Duljaj)	
Ivic	6
Subbed: 87 mins (Stojakovic)	
Tomic ▢	6
Booked: 75 mins (foul)	
Obradovic	5
Subbed: 63 mins (Baljak 6)	
Pekovic ▢ ☆	8
Booked: 33 mins (foul)	
Stojisavljevic	6
sub: *Baljak*	6
sub: *Duljaj*	6
sub: *Stojakovic*	
Subs not used: Ilic, R, Arnaut, Vukovic, Miskovic.	

MATCH FACTS

Shots On Target
Leeds 7-5 Newcastle

Shots Off Target
Leeds 8-1 Newcastle

Hit Woodwork
Leeds 1-0 Newcastle

Corners
Leeds 4-0 Newcastle

HOW THEY LINED UP

Martyn

Kelly Woodgate Radebe Harte

Bakke Batty Bowyer Kewell

Bridges Smith

Ketsbaia Shearer

Solano McClen Speed Dyer

Domi Marcelino Goma Barton

Harper

MATCH FACTS

Shots On Target
Leeds 6-4 Partizan

Shots Off Target
Leeds 4-6 Partizan

Hit Woodwork
Leeds 0-0 Partizan

Corners
Leeds 10-5 Partizan

HOW THEY LINED UP

Martyn

Kelly Radebe Woodgate Harte

Hopkin Batty Bowyer Kewell

Bridges Huckerby

Pekovic Obradovic

Tomic Stanojevic Trobok Stojisavljevic

Savic Ivic Gerasimovski Sabo

Damjanac

29

OCTOBER

"Some people are just getting carried away. It's only October and there's still a long way to go, but the league won't lie. We'll find out in May who the best team is." David O'Leary

OCTOBER OPENED WITH A TRIP TO WATFORD, WHERE ONLY THREE points would do to maintain United's challenge for the title. Graham Taylor's team were struggling at the bottom of the Premiership after being promoted from the First Division and couldn't match an impressive Leeds performance with Bridges and Kewell on target to record United's fifth win on the trot.

Away from the Premiership, Leeds took on Blackburn in the third round of the Worthington Cup. Rovers had been relegated from the top-flight in the previous campaign and started the new season disastrously in Division One. But Brian Kidd's team belied their precarious league position to provide a stern test for The Whites before going down 1-0 to a last-minute goal from Danny Mills. A home fixture in the Premiership followed against Yorkshire rivals Sheffield Wednesday, who were already looking like relegation fodder even at this early stage of the season. But they put in put in in a spirited and committed performance, though United's class eventually told in a 2-0 win.

The victory extended United's winning sequence to nine games – a new club record. The biggest concern for David O'Leary was complacency, but he shouldn't have been worried. The next round of the UEFA Cup against Lokomotiv Moscow – with the first leg in Leeds – looked like a dangerous fixture against an unknown quantity, but the threat never materialised and Leeds notched up a valuable 4-1 lead for the away leg of the tie.

The record sequence finally came to an end in a thrilling 4-4 draw away to Everton, but the team's excellent run of form had still taken them to the top of the Premiership. O'Leary's charges returned to winning ways in the next match – defeating West Ham 1-0. Knowing Leeds had money to spend, the media spent October speculating about new signings, with Leicester City's Emile Heskey repeatedly linked with a £12 million move to Elland Road.

THE GAMES

Oct. 3 v **Watford** (a)

Oct. 13 v **Blackburn** (h)

Oct. 16 v **Sheff. Wed.** (h)

Oct. 21 v **L. Moscow** (h)

Oct. 24 v **Everton** (a)

Oct. 30 v **West Ham** (h)

TRANSFERS IN

None

TRANSFERS OUT

Bruno Ribeiro

Position: **Midfielder**

Fee: **£500,000**

To: **Sheffield United**

MATCH facts
Matchman Of The Month

HARRY KEWELL
Average Rating: 7.50

31

United had too much firepower for Graham Taylor's Watford.

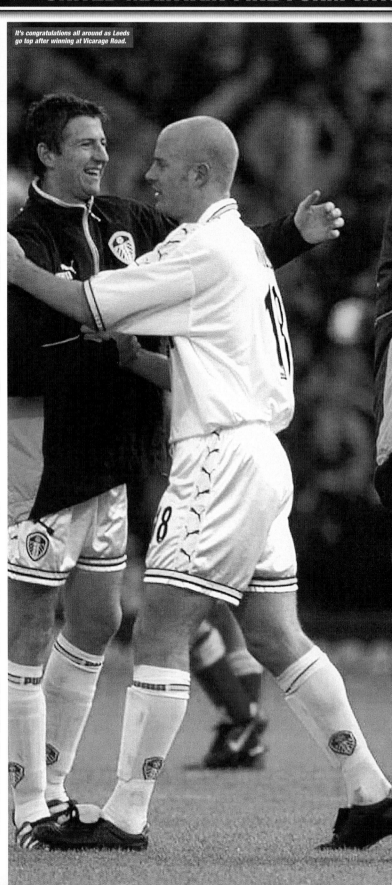

It's congratulations all around as Leeds go top after winning at Vicarage Road.

FROM THE PAGES OF *MATCH*

There haven't been any new additions to the Elland Road trophy cabinet since **DAVID BATTY** left **LEEDS** in 1993, so on his return to the club he set his sights on putting that right for 1999-2000.

Has the club changed much since you left? *"Yeah, but I always wanted to come back while I still had a few years left in me and if I'd missed my chance when it came I don't think I'd have got back here. The time was right and David O'Leary was really keen for me to sign. I'm looking forward to the next few years."*

What do you make of David O'Leary as a boss? *"He's earned a lot of admiration from the lads for the way he's gone about the job. He's there for the players and that's why we work so hard for for him."*

Is he right in playing the club's talented youngsters? *"This season will be a big test for them but I think they've got the right attitude, which is so important. They're all willing to learn and I think there are great things on the horizon for Leeds."*

You're playing more exciting football now aren't you? *"I've had friends go down to watch Leeds play since I've been away from the club and they've come back and told me it was a poor game, but that the team scraped a result. But there's more to football than that – it is entertainment after all. I think David O'Leary is playing the right way – to entertain, but also to get success."*

| Watford | (1) 1 |
| Leeds United | (1) 2 |

Competition: FA Carling Premiership

Date: Sunday October 3, 1999

Attendance: 19,677

Referee: P D'Urso (Billericay) 6

Game 12

THE GAME: Watford took the lead with six minutes left in the first half, but Michael Bridges snatched a fine equaliser on the stroke of half-time. Leeds stepped up a gear after the break, with Harry Kewell enjoying acres of free space on the left of midfield. Nordin Wooter shone for the home side, but Watford were subjected to a bombardment and Kewell got the winning goal that his Man Of The Match performance deserved.

WATFORD GOAL: Williams *(41 mins):* Turned superbly on receiving the ball and hammered his shot past Martyn.

LEEDS GOALS: Bridges *(45 mins):* The Watford defence went absent without leave, allowing Bridges to find the net with a great strike from outside the box; **Kewell** *(69 mins):* Collected the ball on the left and fired a fierce drive which Chamberlain could only help into the Watford net.

MATCH RATING ★★★ LEAGUE POSITION: 1st

> "There are no prizes for being top now, though it's better than being bottom. I'm a young man learning my trade and I just take every game as it comes." DAVID O'LEARY

WATFORD		LEEDS UNITED	
Chamberlain	6	Martyn	6
Lyttle	6	Kelly	6
Subbed: 46 mins (Gibbs)		Batty	7
Page ▯	7	Woodgate	7
Booked: 66 mins (dissent)		Harte ▯	7
Williams ⚽	6	*Booked: 74 mins (foul)*	
Goal: 41 mins		Radebe	6
Robinson ▯	6	*Subbed: 42 mins (Mills)*	
Booked: 53 mins (foul)		Bakke	6
Hyde	6	Hopkin	7
Palmer	7	*Subbed: 86 mins (Haaland)*	
Kennedy	5	Kewell ⚽	☆ 8
Subbed: 80 mins (Easton)		*Goal: 69 mins*	
Ngonge	6	Bridges ⚽	7
Foley	6	*Goal: 45 mins; Subbed: 69 mins*	
Subbed: 69 mins (Miller)		*(Huckerby)*	
Wooter	☆ 8	Smith	6
sub: Gibbs	7	sub: Mills	6
sub: Miller	6	sub: Huckerby	6
sub: Easton		sub: Haaland	
Subs not used: Wright, Day.		*Subs not used: Robinson, Jones.*	

MATCH FACTS

Shots On Target
Watford 5-11 Leeds

Shots Off Target
Watford 6-11 Leeds

Hit Woodwork
Watford 0-0 Leeds

Corners
Watford 5-8 Leeds

HOW THEY LINED UP

Chamberlain

Lyttle Williams Page Robinson

Wooter Palmer Hyde Kennedy

Ngonge Foley

Smith Bridges

Kewell Batty Bakke Hopkin

Harte Radebe Woodgate Kelly

Martyn

IN THE NEWS

LEEDS UNITED: The second leg win over Partizan Belgrade is United's sixth in a row -- the best winning sequence Leeds have had for 26 years, and United's young team are being lauded as the country's in-form team... David O'Leary celebrates his first year in charge at Elland Road by steering his promising side to the top of the Premiership table after the win over Watford... Leeds learn they will face Locomotiv Moscow in the next round of the UEFA Cup and are installed as fifth favourites to win the competition, behind Italians giants Juventus, who are heavily tipped by the bookies.

PREMIERSHIP: David Beckham has been fined two weeks' wages for attending a party at London Fashion Week just 48 hours before Man. United's Champions League encounter with Sturm Graz. The United star has also been called to the FA to discuss his behaviour on the pitch... Former Man. United defender **Steve Bruce** announces the end of his professional playing career after 737 games... **Benito Carbone** turns down a switch to Derby, but Sheffield Wednesday are keen to sell the striker before he is able to move on a free transfer... Italian playmaker **Roberto Baggio** is rumoured to be wanted by Gianluca Vialli at Chelsea.

THE FINAL SCORE!

OCTOBER 2		
Aston Villa	0-0	Liverpool
Bradford	0-4	**Sunderland**
Everton	1-1	Coventry
Sheff.Wed.	5-1	Wimbledon

OCTOBER 3		
Chelsea	5-0	Man. United
Newcastle	2-1	Middlesbrough
Tottenham	2-3	Leicester
Watford	1-2	**Leeds**
West Ham	2-1	Arsenal

TOP OF THE PREMIERSHIP

	P	W	D	L	Pts
1. Leeds	10	7	1	2	22
2. Man. United	10	6	3	1	21
3. Sunderland	10	6	2	2	20
4. Chelsea	8	6	1	1	19

33

Leeds United (0) 1
Blackburn Rovers (0) 0

Competition: Worthington Cup 3rd Rd

Date: Wednesday October 13, 1999

Attendance: 24,353

Referee: J Winter (Stockton) 7

Game 13

THE GAME: Leeds United were riding high at the top of the Premiership and at home to First Division Blackburn Rovers for this Worthington Cup clash. But it took a last-gasp winner from Danny Mills to foil Blackburn and spare United's blushes. Rovers boss Brian Kidd had been forced to field a team full of youngsters at Elland Road because of a crippling injury list, and his side held out well away from home until the winner in the 90th minute from Mills. Extra-time had looked a certainty, with Leeds failing to capitalise on the midfield promptings of David Batty. United missed their in-form dynamo Lee Bowyer, who was injured, and were grateful to be safely through to the next round of the competition.

LEEDS GOALS: Mills *(90 mins):* McPhail sent a throughball for Huckerby to run on to, but the frontman was cynically brought down by Rovers defender Short fractionally outside the penalty area. Mills stepped up and drove the free-kick under 'keeper Filan's body and just inside the near post.

MATCH RATING ★★ LEAGUE POSITION: 1st

"There are times when, for whatever reason, you are not playing well — and in those times you have to make sure that you don't lose." DAVID O'LEARY

LEEDS UNITED	
Martyn	6
Mills ⊕	6
Goal: 90mins	
Radebe	7
Woodgate	7
Kelly	6
Bakke	6
Batty	☆ 8
Hopkin	5
Subbed: 46 mins (McPhail)	
Kewell	4
Bridges	5
Subbed: 46 mins (Huckerby)	
Smith ▢	6
Booked: 52 mins (foul)	
sub: Huckerby	5
sub: McPhail	6

Subs not used: Haaland, Jones, Robinson.

BLACKBURN ROVERS	
Filan	7
Kenna	6
Short	7
Taylor	7
Richardson	6
Johnson	6
Dunn	6
Gill	6
Duff	7
Jansen	☆ 8
Ward	6

Subs not used: Corbett, Grayson, Kelly, Ostenstad, Brown.

MATCH FACTS	
Shots On Target	
Leeds 7-3 Blackburn	
Shots Off Target	
Leeds 4-3 Blackburn	
Hit Woodwork	
Leeds 1-0 Blackburn	
Corners	
Leeds 6-5 Blackburn	

HOW THEY LINED UP

Martyn
Mills — Woodgate — Radebe — Kelly
Hopkin — Batty — Bakke — Kewell
Bridges — Smith
Jansen — Ward
Duff — Gill — Dunn — Johnson
Richardson — Taylor — Short — Kenna
Filan

Leeds did just enough to beat Blackburn's young team.

Bridges has established himself as Elland Road's number one striker.

Leeds United (0) 2
Sheffield Wednesday (0) 0

Competition: FA Carling Premiership

Date: **Saturday October 16, 1999**

Attendance: **39,437**

Referee: **G Barber** (Tring) 7

Game 14

THE GAME: Wednesday's mini-revival came to an abrupt end as Leeds struck late on to equal the club record of nine successive victories, set way back in 1931. Wednesday must still be kicking themselves after missing a host of first-half chances, with Gilles de Bilde, Andy Booth and Danny Sonner all guilty of failing to find the net. Leeds stuttered through the match, only showing patches of their best form in the closing stages. Darren Huckerby, on as a sub for Michael Bridges, played a big part in setting up two goals for Alan Smith, who was more than happy to accept his simple chances.

LEEDS GOALS: Smith (72 mins): Huckerby's shot from just outside the penalty box was fumbled by 'keeper Srnicek, and Smith was on the spot to prod the ball over the line from just inside the six-yard area; **Smith** (78 mins): Huckerby was again the provider, crossing the ball in low from the left to Bowyer, who crashed his effort against the near post from ten yards. Smith showed predatory instincts, lurking a couple of yards out, to pick up the pieces and grab his second to make it 2-0.

MATCH RATING ★★★ **LEAGUE POSITION: 1st**

MATCH FACTS

Shots On Target
Leeds 6-5 Sheff. Wed

Shots Off Target
Leeds 14-9 Sheff. Wed

Hit Woodwork
Leeds 1-0 Sheff. Wed

Corners
Leeds 1-3 Sheff. Wed

HOW THEY LINED UP

Martyn

Mills — Woodgate — Radebe — Kelly

Bowyer — Batty — McPhail — Kewell

Bridges — Smith

de Bilde — Booth

Rudi — Sonner — Jonk — Alexandersson

Hinchcliffe — Thome — Walker — Atherton

Srnicek

LEEDS UNITED

Martyn	7
Mills	5
Radebe	7
Woodgate	7
Kelly	6
Batty	7
Bowyer	6
McPhail	5
Kewell ▯	6
Booked: 70 mins (foul)	
Bridges ▯	5
Booked: 57 mins (foul); Subbed: 62 mins (Huckerby)	
Smith ⊕ ⊕	7
Goals: 72, 78 mins	
sub: Huckerby	☆8

Subs not used: Haaland, Hopkin, Robinson, Bakke.

SHEFFIELD WEDNESDAY

Srnicek	6
Atherton ▯	7
Booked: 18 mins (foul)	
Walker	☆8
Thome	7
Hinchcliffe	7
Alexandersson	7
Sonner ▯	6
Booked: 70 mins (foul)	
Jonk	7
Rudi ▯	6
Booked: 26 mins (foul)	
Booth	6
de Bilde	6

Subs not used: Sibon, Cresswell, Nolan, Briscoe, Pressman.

TOP OF THE PREMIERSHIP

	P	W	D	L	Pts
1. Leeds	11	8	1	2	25
2. Man. United	11	7	3	1	24
3. Arsenal	11	7	1	3	22
4. Sunderland	10	6	2	2	20

Alan Smith scores an acrobatic third goal in United's convincing 4-1 win.

Harry Kewell was getting to like big European nights.

| Leeds United | (2) | **4** |
| Lokomotiv Moscow | (0) | **1** |

Competition: UEFA Cup 2nd Rd 1st Leg

Date: Thursday October 21, 1999

Attendance: 37, 814

Referee: W Stark (Germany) 7

 Game 15

THE GAME: Lee Bowyer gave a spellbinding midfield display as Lokomotiv Moscow were crushed by a Leeds side at the peak of their form. The England Under-21 star struck twice to soften up the Russians before Alan Smith added a third early in the second half. The outstanding Lokomotiv player was Dmitri Loskov, who forced two great saves from Nigel Martyn, and he finally beat the Leeds 'keeper with a viciously swerving free-kick to give the Russian team hope. But Harry Kewell soon restored his side's three-goal cushion as United cruised to a comfortable victory at Elland Road. It must be getting difficult for England coach Kevin Keegan to ignore Bowyer's claims for a promotion to the senior squad.

LEEDS GOALS: Bowyer (27 mins): Bridges rose beyond the far post to meet McPhail's free-kick from the left of the area. Woodgate, a yard out, turned the ball back for the on-rushing Bowyer to strike a shot just inside the left post from 13 yards, with the ball taking a slight deflection on its way into the net; **Bowyer** (45 mins): From inside his own half, Bowyer picked out Bridges on the left before making a strong run into the penalty area. He was perfectly positioned to head powerfully past the startled 'keeper when Bridges crossed the ball back to him; **Smith** (56 mins): Lokomotiv goalkeeper Nigmatullin flapped at Kelly's right-wing cross while under pressure from Bridges. Smith was quickest to react with a surprise overhead kick from six yards; **Kewell** (83 mins): Substitute Huckerby made ground down the right and sent over a deep cross to Kewell on the far side of the penalty area. The Australian star unleashed a ferocious shot into the net from 14 yards.

LOKOMOTIV GOAL: Loskov (81 mins): Radebe was harshly judged to have fouled Boulykin just outside United's area and Loskov's curling free-kick beat Martyn's despairing dive.

MATCH RATING ★★★ **LEAGUE POSITION: 1st**

MATCH FACTS
Shots On Target
Leeds 7-4 Lokomotiv
Shots Off Target
Leeds 8-9 Lokomotiv
Hit Woodwork
Leeds 0-1 Lokomotiv
Corners
Leeds 10-2 Lokomotiv

LEEDS UNITED
Martyn	8
Kelly	7
Radebe	8
Booked: 80 mins (foul)	
Woodgate	7
Harte	7
Bowyer ⊕⊕	☆ 9
Goals: 27, 45 mins	
Batty	8
McPhail	6
Kewell ⊕	7
Goal: 83 mins	
Smith ⊕	7
Goal: 56 mins	
Bridges	7
Subbed: 62 mins (Huckerby)	
sub: Huckerby	7

Subs not used: Haaland, Hopkin, Jones, Robinson, Mills, Bakke.

LOKOMOTIV MOSCOW
Nigmatullin	5
Arifdoline	7
Drozdov	6
Booked: 75 mins (foul)	
Kharlatchev	7
Lavrik	6
Tchougainov	7
Smertin	7
Pachinine	6
Subbed: 61 mins (Hovhannisyan)	
Janashia	6
Subbed: 39 mins (Boulykin)	
Loskov ⊕	☆ 8
Goal: 81 mins	
Sarkisian	6
Subbed: 76 mins (Maminov)	
sub: Boulykin	7
sub: Hovhannisyan	6
sub: Maminov	6

Subs not used: Poliakov, Neretine, Solomatin, Semenenko.

HOW THEY LINED UP

Martyn

Kelly Woodgate Radebe Harte

McPhail Batty Bowyer Kewell

Bridges Smith

Janashia Loskov

Sarkisian Pashinine Tchougainov Smertin

Lavrik Kharlatchev Drozdov Arifdoline

Nigmatullin

Woodgate thought he had grabbed the winner to make it 4-3 to Leeds.

Everton (3) 4
Leeds United (2) 4

Competition: FA Carling Premiership

Date: **Sunday October 24, 1999**

Attendance: **37,355**

Referee: **D Gallagher** (Banbury) 7

Game 16

THE GAME: Leeds failed to record their 11th victory in a row after a thrilling 4-4 draw at Goodison Park. Everton started the game in positive fashion and took the lead against the league leaders on three occasions. The game was played at a terrific pace, with both sets of strikers on top form. Unfortunately, the defending on both sides was less than impressive, but it was still compelling to watch. Leeds took the lead for the first time 20 minutes before the end through Woodgate's header, then shut up shop to go for all three points, but they were unable to prevent a dramatic last-gasp equaliser from David Weir.

EVERTON GOALS: Campbell *(4 mins):* Broke clear from the Leeds defence to hit a right-footed curling shot from 15 yards; **Campbell** *(28 mins):* Barmby sent a throughball to Campbell, who blasted the ball past Martyn; **Hutchison** *(37 mins):* Put Everton back in the lead after the ball pinged around the area and rebounded for Hutchison to bundle the ball home; **Weir** *(90 mins):* Unsworth crossed left-footed to Weir, who headed home to make it 4-4 and secure a point for the Merseysiders.

LEEDS GOALS: Bridges *(15 mins):* A cross by Kewell found Bridges unmarked in acres of space, gifting the striker an easy tap-in from five yards; **Kewell** *(35 mins):* Scored with a bizarre cross-shot from 40 yards out, which looped over the stranded goalkeeper Gerrard; **Bridges** *(68 mins):* A spectacular lob from 25 yards out on the right-hand touchline; **Woodgate** *(72 mins):* The centre-back was given too much space in the area by the tired Everton defence and fired a solid header into the net.

MATCH RATING ★★★★ **LEAGUE POSITION: 1st**

EVERTON

Gerrard	6
Ball	7
Subbed: 79 mins (Johnson)	
Gough	7
Watson	6
Unsworth	6
Weir ⊕	7
Goal: 90 mins	
Barmby	7
Collins	☆ 8
Gemmill	6
Subbed: 27 mins (Pembridge)	
Hutchison ⊕	7
Goal: 37 mins	
Campbell ⊕ ⊕	8
Goals: 4, 28 mins	
sub: Pembridge	5
sub: Johnson	5

Subs not used: Cadamarteri, Ward, Simonsen.

LEEDS UNITED

Martyn	6
Kelly	7
Harte	7
Radebe	6
Woodgate ⊕	6
Goal: 72 mins	
Bridges ⊕ ⊕	☆ 8
Goal: 15, 68 mins	
Kewell ⊕	8
Goal: 35 mins	
Bowyer	7
McPhail	6
Smith	7
(sub 67 mins Huckerby 6)	
Batty	6
sub: Huckerby	6

Subs not used: Hopkin, Haaland, Robinson, Mills.

MATCH FACTS	HOW THEY LINED UP
Shots On Target	
Everton 8-9 Leeds	
Shots Off Target	
Everton 9-8 Leeds	
Hit Woodwork	
Everton 0-0 Leeds	
Corners	
Everton 8-8 Leeds	

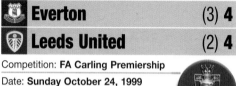

HOW THEY LINED UP

Gerrard

Weir · Gough · Watson · Unsworth · Ball

Gemmill · Collins · Barmby

Hutchison · Campbell

Smith · Bridges

Kewell · McPhail · Batty · Bowyer

Harte · Radebe · Woodgate · Kelly

Martyn

 Leeds United (0) **1**

 West Ham United (0) **0**

Competition: **FA Carling Premiership**

Date: **Saturday October 30, 1999**

Attendance: **40,190**

Referee: **G Poll** (Tring) 6

 Game 17

THE GAME: David O'Leary's side rarely showed the sort of form they need to maintain a serious title challenge. Despite having the lion's share of possession at Elland Road, Leeds struggled to create many genuine goalscoring chances and were often restricted to speculative long range attempts from the industrious Harry Kewell. United made it 12 successive games unbeaten though, while The Hammers suffered their sixth straight away defeat in the Premiership. The Londoners came close to a point, with Frank Lampard peppering Nigel Martyn's goal with a succession of late shots. But it was too little too late for West Ham, who ultimately suffered for their lack of adventure for the majority of the match.

LEEDS GOALS: Harte *(57 mins):* Bowyer played the ball into the goalmouth, where Lomas headed out to Harte. The Leeds left-back collected the ball from just inside the penalty box and curled a right-foot shot just inside Hislop's near post.

MATCH RATING ★★★ LEAGUE POSITION: 1st

> "It is hard because there's been some ridiculous hype surrounding Leeds. It has put a lot of pressure on the young players and I don't think we are ready to win the league yet." DARREN HUCKERBY

LEEDS UNITED	
Martyn	7
Kelly	7
Radebe	7
Woodgate	7
Harte ⚽	7
Goal: 57 mins	
Bowyer ▯	6
Booked: 45 mins (foul)	
Batty	7
Kewell ☆	8
McPhail	7
Smith	6
Subbed: 58 mins (Huckerby)	
Bridges ▯	7
Booked: 58 mins (foul)	
sub: Huckerby	7

Subs not used: Hopkin, Robinson, Mills, Bakke.

WEST HAM UNITED	
Hislop	6
Ferdinand	7
Ruddock ☆	8
Margas	6
Lomas ▯	7
Booked: 51 mins (time-wasting)	
Foe ▯	6
Booked: 45 mins (foul); Subbed: 70 mins (Cole)	
Lampard	7
Moncur ▯	6
Booked: 3 mins (unsporting behaviour)	
Keller	6
Wanchope	6
Kitson	5
sub: Cole	7

Subs not used: Potts, Carrick, Newton, Forrest.

MATCH FACTS
Shots On Target
Leeds 5-4 West Ham
Shots Off Target
Leeds 8-4 West Ham
Hit Woodwork
Leeds 0-0 West Ham
Corners
Leeds 16-4 West Ham

HOW THEY LINED UP
Martyn
Kelly Woodgate Radebe Harte
Bowyer Batty McPhail Kewell
Smith Bridges
Kitson Wanchope
Keller Foe Lampard Moncur Lomas
Ferdinand Margas Ruddock
Hislop

IN THE NEWS
LEEDS UNITED: The latest striker to be linked with a move to Elland Road is Leicester's **Emile Heskey**, with David O'Leary believed to be preparing a £12 million offer... **Lee Bowyer** is refusing to undergo a groin operation, sensing United could be in the midst of a very special season – he says he'll put it off until the summer break... David O'Leary is angered by 'fans' who are giving United players a hard time after some indifferent displays, even though Leeds are on an impressive unbeaten streak.

PREMIERSHIP: Aston Villa sign Italian striker **Benito Carbone** until the end of the 1999-2000 season, when he becomes a free agent... A group of Newcastle season ticket holders stage a protest at plans to either move their seating positions next season or face paying three times the old price to retain their seats... Liverpool striker **Michael Owen** limps off only eight minutes after coming on as a substitute in the draw with Southampton... Arsenal legend **Ian Wright** joins Celtic on loan from West Ham in an attempt to help solve the Glasgow side's striking problems.

THE FINAL SCORE!
OCTOBER 23
Aston Villa	1-1	Wimbledon
Bradford	3-1	Leicester
Chelsea	2-3	**Arsenal**
Sheff. Wed.	0-0	Coventry
Southampton	1-1	Liverpool
Tottenham	3-1	Man. United

OCTOBER 24
Everton	4-4	Leeds
Watford	1-2	**Middlesbrough**
West Ham	1-1	Sunderland

OCTOBER 25
Newcastle	2-0	Derby

OCTOBER 27
Liverpool	1-0	West Ham

OCTOBER 30
Arsenal	0-0	Newcastle
Derby	3-1	Chelsea
Leeds	1-0	West Ham
Leicester	3-0	Sheff. Wed.
Man. United	3-0	Aston Villa
Middlesbrough	2-1	Everton
Wimbledon	1-1	Southampton

OCTOBER 31
Coventry	4-0	Watford
Sunderland	2-1	Tottenham

TOP OF THE PREMIERSHIP
	P	W	D	L	Pts
1. Leeds	13	9	2	2	29
2. Arsenal	13	8	3	2	27
3. Man. United	13	8	2	3	26
4. Sunderland	13	8	3	2	27

NOVEMBER

"There aren't many teams who can show form like ours when we get going. I'm happy with the way the team's playing and I've kept my place in the team." Stephen McPhail

DESPITE LEEDS' FANTASTIC FORM, DAVID O'LEARY WAS HAPPY TO
be written off by the critics. He agreed that his side needed more experience and pointed out that his squad also lacked strength in depth – but whether he really believed this was open to question. By refusing to add to the hype about his players he helped them to ignore it and get on with their task.

European football was proving to be an enjoyable experience for Leeds. The team was full of confidence after taking a 4-1 lead against Lokomotiv Moscow in the first leg of the UEFA Cup tie at Elland Road. The second leg in Russia was comfortable for United, who added three goals in the first half to make it 7-1 on aggregate. But with a host of top teams dropping out of the Champions League and being entered into the UEFA Cup third round draw, The Whites couldn't afford to relax. David O'Leary didn't agree with the rules that allowed teams to fail in one European competition but take part in another. The Leeds chief didn't believe that the likes of Juventus, Galatasaray and Arsenal had any right to go straight into the third round of the UEFA Cup as a reward for Champions League defeat.

November threw up some of the season's more uncomplicated fixtures for Leeds in the Premiership, but as they were top of the league and in terrific form, they didn't need to fear playing anyone anyway. Lowly Wimbledon, Bradford and Southampton were the opposition for November – but not everything went according to plan. Wimbledon shocked the Premiership leaders by claiming all three points in a 2-0 win at Selhurst Park.

After the loss to Wimbledon, which had knocked them off top spot, United hit back in the best way possible. They secured a 2-1 win against Bradford then completed their first double win of the season – against Southampton – to show that O'Leary's youngsters would be a match for anyone.

THE GAMES

Nov. 4 v **L. Moscow** (a)
Nov. 7 v **Wimbledon** (a)
Nov. 20 v **Bradford** (h)
Nov. 28 v **Southampton** (h)

TRANSFERS IN

None

TRANSFERS OUT

Danny Granville
Position: **Defender**
Fee: **Undisclosed**
To: **Manchester City**

MATCH*facts*

Matchman Of The Month

DAVID BATTY
Average Rating: 7.00

JONATHAN WOODGATE
Average Rating: 7.00

Two goals from Bridges smoothed United's passage into the third round of the UEFA Cup.

Egil Olsen's Wimbledon caused the upset of the day by beating the Premiership leaders.

Lokomotiv Moscow (0) 0
Leeds United (3) 3

Leeds win 7-1 on aggregate.

Competition: **UEFA Cup 2nd Rd 2nd Leg**

Date: **Thursday November 4, 1999**

Attendance: **4,000**

Referee: **A Sars** (France) 7

Game 18

THE GAME: David O'Leary's young side flew into Moscow with a 4-1 lead after a cracking victory against the Russians in the first leg at Elland Road two weeks earlier. The manager must have thought that a tight defensive display was required for his side to progress to the third round of the UEFA Cup. But with only three minutes on the clock, Boulykin was guilty of a missed chance and the home team could have been two goals up early on. The game changed when a reckless tackle on Harry Kewell earned Leeds a penalty, and from then on it became a formality, with United eventually running out 7-1 aggregate winners. Leeds fans know the European games will get harder from now on, with teams that have been knocked out of the Champions League, such as Juventus and Arsenal, included in the draw for the next round of the competition.

LEEDS GOALS: Harte *(penalty 15 mins):* A neat flick from Bridges allowed Kewell to burst into the penalty area, only to be brought down by Arifdoline. Harte stepped up and coolly slotted the ball into the right-hand corner, sending the 'keeper the wrong way; **Bridges** *(26 mins):* Harte swung in a deep cross to the back post, allowing Bowyer to expertly flick the ball back across the six-yard box for the onrushing Bridges to score neatly from two yards out; **Bridges** *(44 mins):* A long ball was played over Moscow's defence and Bridges ran on to slot the ball into the far right-hand corner, past the despairing dive of 'keeper Nigamtoulline.

MATCH RATING ★★★ LEAGUE POSITION: 1st

LOKOMOTIV MOSCOW

Nigmatullin	5
Arifdoline	5
Lavrik	6
Pashinine	6
Ovannesyan	6
Subbed: 77 mins (Semenenko)	
Tchougainov	6
Smertin	7
Boulykin	6
Subbed: 74 mins (Piminov)	
Loskov ☆	7
Sarkisian	6
Solomatin 🟨	6
Booked: 46 mins (foul)	
sub: Piminov	
sub: Semenenko	

Subs not used: Poliakov, Kharlachev, Maminov, Neretine.

LEEDS UNITED

Martyn	7
Kelly 🟨	6
Booked: 87 mins (foul)	
Radebe 🟨	7
Booked: 40 mins (foul)	
Woodgate	7
Harte ⚽	7
Goal: 15 mins	
Bowyer	6
Subbed: 46 mins (Haaland)	
Batty	7
McPhail	7
Subbed: 80 mins (Hopkin)	
Kewell	8
Subbed: 65 mins (Huckerby)	
Bridges ⚽⚽ ☆	8
Goals: 26, 44 mins	
Bakke 🟨	7
Booked: 51 mins (foul)	
sub: Haaland	6
sub: Huckerby	6
sub: Hopkin	

Subs not used: Robinson, Mills, Duberry, Smith.

MATCH FACTS

Shots On Target
Lokomotiv 6-8 Leeds

Shots Off Target
Lokomotiv 10-5 Leeds

Hit Woodwork
Lokomotiv 0-0 Leeds

Corners
Lokomotiv 5-3 Leeds

HOW THEY LINED UP

Nigmatullin

Arifdoline Lavrik Ovannesyan Solomatin

Smertin Tchougainov Pashinine Sarkisian

Loskov Boulykin

Bridges

Kewell McPhail Bakke Batty Bowyer

Harte Radebe Woodgate Kelly

Martyn

 # Wimbledon (1) 2
Leeds United (0) 0

Competition: FA Carling Premiership
Date: Sunday November 7, 1999
Attendance: 18,747
Referee: P Jones (Loughborough) 7

 Game 19

THE GAME: After their champagne performance in the UEFA Cup in Moscow on Thursday night, United's bubble was well and truly burst by Wimbledon at Selhurst Park. Leeds looked tired after their European exploits and they were disappointing in trying to regain top spot in the Premiership, having lost their lead to Manchester United a day earlier. Wimbledon defended resolutely in the first half, often calling seven players back into the penalty area to form two lines of defence. Ben Thatcher had a superb game – repeatedly emerging from defence with the ball to defy Leeds as they pushed forward. The second half was a different story in which The Dons took the initiative, pinning United back for long periods – despite the efforts of the industrious David Batty to get Leeds back into the game. The in-form striker Michael Bridges, who didn't play because of a back injury, was sorely missed up front.

WIMBLEDON GOALS: Hartson (30 mins): Hammered in his seventh goal of the season with a low, hard shot from 15 yards following a move involving team-mates Earle and Euell; Gayle (65 mins): Headed home a good Kimble corner after Leeds defender Radebe had almost conceded an own goal by heading narrowly wide of his own post.

MATCH RATING ★★★ LEAGUE POSITION: 2nd

WIMBLEDON	
Sullivan	7
Cunningham	7
Kimble	7
Booked: 25 mins (foul)	
Thatcher	☆ 8
Cort	6
Subbed: 89 mins (Andreson)	
Earle	8
Hartson	7
Goal: 30 mins; Subbed: 88 mins (Leaburn)	
Euell	7
Gayle	8
Goal: 65 mins; Subbed: 80 mins (Badir)	
Andersen	7
Hreidarsson	7
Booked: 50 mins (dissent)	
sub: *Badir*	
sub: *Leaburn*	
sub: *Andreson*	

Subs not used: Blackwell, Davis.

LEEDS UNITED	
Martyn	7
Kelly	7
Harte	6
Radebe	7
Woodgate	6
Subbed: 46 mins (Duberry)	
Kewell	7
Bowyer	5
Subbed: 61 mins (Bakke)	
Huckerby	7
McPhail	7
Smith	7
Subbed: 78 mins (Hopkin)	
Batty	☆ 8
sub: *Duberry*	7
sub: *Bakke*	7
sub: *Hopkin*	

Subs not used: Robinson, Mills.

MATCH FACTS
Shots On Target
Wimbledon 4-9 Leeds
Shots Off Target
Wimbledon 6-3 Leeds
Hit Woodwork
Wimbledon 0-0 Leeds
Corners
Wimbledon 4-10 Leeds

HOW THEY LINED UP

Sullivan

Kimble — Cunningham — Hreidarsson — Thatcher

Andersen — Earle — Euell — Gayle

Hartson — Cort

Smith — Huckerby

Kewell — McPhail — Batty — Bowyer

Harte — Radebe — Woodgate — Kelly

Martyn

THE FINAL SCORE!

NOVEMBER 7

Chelsea	0-0	West Ham
Newcastle	1-1	Everton
Tottenham	2-1	Arsenal
Wimbledon	2-0	Leeds

TOP OF THE PREMIERSHIP

	P	W	D	L	Pts
1. Man. United	14	9	3	2	30
2. Leeds	14	9	2	3	29
3. Sunderland	14	8	4	2	28
4. Arsenal	14	8	2	4	26

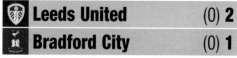
Leeds made sure that Bradford's dismal run at Elland Road continued.

Leeds United (0) 2
Bradford City (0) 1

Competition: FA Carling Premiership

Date: Saturday November 20, 1999

Attendance: 39,937

Referee: P Durkin (Portland) 6

Game 20

THE GAME: Bradford City had never won a league game at Elland Road before and Leeds made certain their neighbours' dismal run continued into the next century. Bradford hung on bravely with David Wetherall, Lee Sharpe and Gunnar Halle defending doggedly against their former club, but once Alan Smith had broken the deadlock nine minutes into the second half, the destiny of the points was rarely in doubt. Goalkeeper Matt Clarke experienced a busy afternoon between the posts for Bradford and the deficit would have been much greater if he hadn't been in inspired form. Bradford battled hard though, conceding a string of bookings in their struggle to keep Leeds at bay. Their late goal set up a tense final few seconds, but United should have made the game safe well before then.

LEEDS GOALS: Smith *(54 mins):* Bridges shot low into the goalmouth from the right side of the penalty area and Smith stuck out a boot just ahead of Wetherall, sending the ball looping over 'keeper Clarke; **Harte** *(penalty 80 mins):* McCall played a short backpass which caused panic in The Bantams' defence, then Clarke collided with Bowyer and brought down the onrushing Batty. Harte stepped up to send an assured penalty-kick into the bottom left-hand corner of the net.

BRADFORD GOAL: Windass *(90 mins):* Slack marking on the Leeds right enabled Windass to weave through the Leeds defence before skipping round 'keeper Martyn and scoring.

MATCH RATING ★★★ LEAGUE POSITION: 2nd

LEEDS UNITED

Martyn	7
Kelly	6
Radebe	☆ 8
Woodgate	7
Harte ⊕	7
Goal: 80 mins	
Bakke	7
McPhail	7
Batty	7
Bowyer ▢	6
Booked: 87 mins (foul)	
Bridges	5
Smith ⊕	6
Goal: 54 mins; Subbed: 76 mins (Huckerby)	
sub: *Huckerby*	

Subs not used: Hopkin, Mills, Duberry, Robinson.

BRADFORD CITY

Clarke	7
Halle	6
Wetherall	☆ 8
O'Brien	7
Sharpe ▢	6
Booked: 56 mins (foul)	
Lawrence	6
Windass ▢ ⊕	7
Booked: 60 mins (foul); Goal: 90 mins	
McCall ▢	7
Booked: 40 mins (foul)	
Redfearn	6
Subbed: 64 mins (Blake)	
Beagrie	7
Subbed: 78 mins (Myers)	
Mills ▢	6
Booked: 14 mins (foul)	
sub: *Blake*	7
sub: *Myers*	

Subs not used: Westwood, Whalley, Walsh.

MATCH FACTS

Shots On Target
Leeds 7-5 Bradford

Shots Off Target
Leeds 7-9 Bradford

Hit Woodwork
Leeds 1-0 Bradford

Corners
Leeds 10-4 Bradford

HOW THEY LINED UP

Clarke

Halle — Wetherall — O'Brien — Sharpe

Lawrence — McCall — Redfearn — Beagrie

Windass — Mills

Smith — Bridges

McPhail — Batty — Bakke — Bowyer

Harte — Woodgate — Radebe — Kelly

Martyn

 Leeds United (0) **1**

 Southampton (0) **0**

Competition: FA Carling Premiership

Date: Sunday November 28, 1999

Attendance: 39,288

Referee: R Harris (Oxford) 6

 Game 21

THE GAME: Michael Bridges gunned down The Saints for the second time this season as Leeds climbed back above Manchester United to regain the top spot in the Premiership. Bridges, who bagged a hat-trick at The Dell back in August, was the scourge of Southampton again, making it four goals in two games against The Saints this season. The visitors must have thought they'd done enough to hang on to earn a point before Bridges popped up on the stroke of full time to notch his 12th goal of the campaign. Leeds were decidely off-form at home and it was a less than convincing win after losing inspirational midfielder David Batty in the first half.

LEEDS GOALS: Bridges (90 mins): Fired home a ferocious, match-winning volley from 16 yards out, which flew past the despairing hand of Jones in the Southampton goal.

MATCH RATING ★★★ LEAGUE POSITION: 1st

> "We dominated the entire game. There was only one team that was ever going to score out there and that was us." DAVID O'LEARY

LEEDS UNITED	
Martyn	7
Kelly	7
Woodgate	☆ 8
Mills	7
Harte	7
Bowyer ▢	6
Booked: 70 mins (foul)	
Batty	6
Subbed: 31 mins (Bakke)	
McPhail	6
Kewell	7
Smith	6
Subbed: 63 mins (Huckerby)	
Bridges ⊕	6
Goal: 90 mins	
sub: Bakke ▢	7
Booked: 52 mins (foul)	
sub: Huckerby	6

Subs not used: Haaland, Hiden, Robinson.

SOUTHAMPTON	
Jones	7
Tessem	6
Lundekvam	7
Richards	7
Colleter ▢ ▮	6
Booked: 58 mins (foul); Sent-off 88 mins (second bookable offence: foul)	
Ripley	6
Soltvedt	6
Hughes, M ▢	7
Booked: 66 mins (foul); Subbed: 77 mins (Beattie)	
Oakley	6
Kachloul ▢	☆ 8
Booked: 30 mins (dissent)	
Pahars ▢	6
Booked: 33 mins (foul); Subbed: 89 mins (Dodd)	
sub: Beattie	
sub: Dodd	

Subs not used: Moss, Le Tissier, Boa Morte.

MATCH FACTS	
Shots On Target	
Leeds 6-2 Southampton	
Shots Off Target	
Leeds 14-3 Southampton	
Hit Woodwork	
Leeds 0-0 Southampton	
Corners	
Leeds 7-4 Southampton	

HOW THEY LINED UP
Martyn
Kelly Woodgate Mills Harte
Bowyer Batty McPhail Kewell
Bridges Smith
Pahars Kachloul
Oakley Soltvedt Hughes Ripley
Colleter Richards Lundekvam Tessem
Jones

IN THE NEWS

LEEDS UNITED: The away leg of United's UEFA Cup tie against Spartak Moscow will be played in the capital after all. The Russians asked for the game be moved to Vladikukaz, which is warmer than Moscow, but UEFA have decided the new venue – which is close to Chechnya – is not suitable as the Chechen capital, Grozny, is being bombed by Russia... FIFA ban **Harry Kewell** from playing against Bradford when the winger decides not to travel to Australia for the friendly against Brazil.

PREMIERSHIP:... Aston Villa's **Gareth Southgate** finds himself on an FA misconduct charge after his first ever sending-off away against Leicester... Derby's Argentina striker **Esteban Fuertes** is banned from re-entering England after his passport is declared to be fake... Arsenal are looking at three sites in London on which to build a new £100 million, 60,000 stadium... Leicester City have abandoned plans to sign Sheffield Wednesday striker **Andy Booth** for £2.7 million because of a dispute over payment of the transfer fee... **Nwankwo Kanu** is expected to sign a new, four-year contract at Arsenal worth an estimated £4 million.

THE FINAL SCORE!

NOVEMBER 20		
Arsenal	5-1	Middlesbrough
Derby	1-2	**Man. United**
Everton	1-1	Chelsea
Leeds	2-1	Bradford
Leicester	2-1	Wimbledon
Southampton	0-1	**Tottenham**
Sunderland	0-2	**Liverpool**
Watford	1-1	Newcastle

NOVEMBER 21		
West Ham	4-3	Sheff. Wed.

NOVEMBER 22		
Coventry	2-1	Aston Villa

NOVEMBER 27		
Coventry	0-1	**Leicester**
Everton	0-0	Aston Villa
Middlesbrough	0-0	Wimbledon
Watford	2-3	**Sunderland**
West Ham	1-0	Liverpool

NOVEMBER 28		
Arsenal	2-1	Derby
Chelsea	1-0	Bradford
Leeds	1-0	Southampton
Newcastle	2-1	Tottenham

TOP OF THE PREMIERSHIP

	P	W	D	L	Pts
1. Leeds	16	11	3	2	36
2. Man. United	15	10	3	2	33
3. Arsenal	16	10	2	4	32
4. Sunderland	16	9	4	3	31

45

DECEMBER

"We're enjoying being at the top. I don't know where we'll finish, but I'd like to think we can stay there – I wish the medals were given out at the half-way stage!" David O'Leary

CHRISTMAS IS TRADITIONALLY A TIME FOR GIVING, BUT FOR LEEDS the festive period took away one of their most influential and experienced players. As the championship race entered a crucial stage, it emerged that inspirational England midfielder David Batty had picked up an ankle injury in the 2-1 win over Bradford in November. His influence over the younger members of the team would be missed, but David O'Leary continued his faith in youth by handing a rare opportunity to Norwegian star Eirik Bakke. The Scandinavian giant proved to be an inspiration, turning in a string of outstanding performances to reduce the impact of Batty's absence.

December was a hectic conveyor belt of matches on four different fronts, with Leeds having to play eight games in 26 days. A 2-1 defeat in the first leg of United's third round UEFA Cup clash against Spartak Moscow was followed by a last-minute 1-0 win over struggling Derby in the Premiership. In the second leg of the UEFA Cup tie, Leeds had to rely on another late strike when Lucas Radebe scored the only goal of the game with just six minutes left to put his side into the fourth round on the away goals rule.

The third round of the FA Cup was next, with Leeds securing a 2-0 victory against First Division strugglers Port Vale. The Worthington Cup wasn't such an easy ride as The Whites were defeated by bogey side Leicester City – the same team that knocked them out of the competition in 1998. After playing 120 minutes without any score, Leicester won the game 4-2 on penalties and sent Leeds crashing out of the competition. Back in the Premiership, The Whites battled to a 2-0 win against Chelsea at Stamford Bridge and wasted no time in avenging their Worthington Cup loss by beating Leicester 2-1 on Boxing Day. After a tiring month, United lost 2-0 against a rampant Arsenal at Highbury, but still finished the year at the top of the Premiership.

THE GAMES

Dec. 2 v **S. Moscow** (a)

Dec. 5 v **Derby** (a)

Dec. 9 v **S. Moscow** (h)

Dec. 12 v **Port Vale** (h)

Dec. 15 v **Leicester** (a)

Dec. 19 v **Chelsea** (a)

Dec. 26 v **Leicester** (h)

Dec. 28 v **Arsenal** (a)

TRANSFERS IN

Jason Wilcox

Position: **Midfielder**

Fee: **£3 million**

From: **Blackburn Rovers**

TRANSFERS OUT

None

MATCH facts

Matchman Of The Month

HARRY KEWELL

Average Rating: 7.25

47

Gary Kelly leads the side out to face Spartak Moscow in Bulgaria.

FROM THE PAGES OF *MATCH*

MICHAEL BRIDGES began 1999 fighting for his place at Sunderland. At the end of the year he was leading United's Premiership title charge. He looked back with **MATCH** on his eventful year.

Has it been a good year then? *"Yeah, this time last year I was competing for a place in the Sunderland first team in Division One and now I'm playing for a very exciting young team that's at the top of the Premiership."*

What's been your personal footy highlight? *"I enjoyed scoring a hat-trick at Southampton in what was my second game for Leeds. On the team coach after the game, I had a smile on my face that lasted all the way back to Leeds!"*

Is there anything you'd change about it? *"No, not really. I did pick up an injury near the end of last season which meant that I couldn't take part in some of the key games for Sunderland and I obviously would have liked to have played in those. It's frustrating to be sitting in the stand watching the game – it's much better to be out there on the pitch."*

What has been your all-time football highlight? *"I think it would have to be when Sunderland won the First Division championship. It was brilliant for all the fans who followed the team everywhere. I hope I can have a good season like that next year with Leeds."*

What was the most annoying thing about your football in 1999? *"The same as it is every year – getting injuries, hitting the woodwork and goalkeepers!"*

Do you have a wish for 2000? *"I would like to score a few more goals and hopefully Leeds can secure a place in next season's Champions League. That would be great, to play against the very best sides in Europe."*

 Spartak Moscow (1) **2**

 Leeds United (1) **1**

Competition: UEFA Cup 3rd Rd 1st Leg

Date: Thursday December 2, 1999

Attendance: 5,485

Referee: A Frisk (Sweden) 6

 Game 22

THE GAME: Spartak Moscow will take a 2-1 advantage into the return leg of this third round tie after their narrow win in Bulgaria. Leeds boss David O'Leary will be disappointed after his side started brightly, taking the lead early on and looking relatively comfortable in the first 20 minutes. However, as the ground hardened in a freezing cold Sofia, so did the home team's resilience. Both Robson and Schirko caused plenty of problems for the Leeds defence and by the end of the match David O'Leary will have been happy to get on the plane with his UEFA Cup dreams still intact. Spartak Moscow failed to convert their superior share of possession into goals, leaving next week's return leg at Elland Road in the balance.

SPARTAK GOALS: Schirko (38 mins): A Spartak corner from the right was swung into Schirko, who showed some excellent control to swivel in front of Bakke and blast his strike between Martyn and his near post to bring the scores level; **Robson** (65 mins): A neat interchange on the edge of the area split the Leeds defence wide open and ended with a ball being played square to Spartak striker Robson, who gratefully tapped in his shot from just six yards out to make it 2-1.

LEEDS GOALS: Kewell (14 mins): A mis-hit backpass by Khlestov allowed Kewell to put Leeds ahead, using his electric pace to nip in and take the ball around goalkeeper Filimonov before easily slotting home left-footed from an acute angle.

MATCH RATING ★★★ LEAGUE POSITION: 3rd

SPARTAK MOSCOW		LEEDS UNITED	
Filimonov	7	Martyn	7
Kovtun 🟨	7	Kelly	6
Booked: 53 mins (foul)		Woodgate	6
Khlestov	6	Duberry	6
Bouschmanov	7	Harte 🟨	6
Baranov	5	*Booked: 81 mins (foul)*	
Bulatov	6	Bakke	6
Titov	7	Bowyer	6
Parfionov	6	McPhail	6
Schirko ⊕	☆8	Haaland	5
Goal: 38 mins		Kewell ⊕	☆7
Bezrodny	7	*Goal: 14 mins*	
Robson ⊕	8	Bridges	7
Goal: 65 mins		*Subbed: 55 mins (Huckerby)*	
		sub: Huckerby	5
Subs not used: Smetanin, Ananko, Kechinov, Evseev, Melyoshin.		**Subs not used:** Robinson, Mills, Maybury, Jones, Hiden, Smith.	

MATCH FACTS	
Shots On Target	
Spartak 10-4 Leeds	
Shots Off Target	
Spartak 8-7 Leeds	
Hit Woodwork	
Spartak 0-1 Leeds	
Corners	
Spartak 9-3 Leeds	

HOW THEY LINED UP

Filimonov

Parfionov Bouschmanov Khlestov Kovton

Baranov Bulatov Titov Bezrodny

Robson Schirko

Kewell Bridges

McPhail Bakke Haaland Bowyer

Harte Duberry Woodgate Kelly

Martyn

THIS WEEK...

IN THE NEWS

LEEDS UNITED: A calf injury which forced **David Batty** off after 30 minutes against Southampton means he doesn't travel to Sofia for the first leg of the UEFA Cup tie against Spartak Moscow. Captain **Lucas Radebe** also misses the game due to suspension... Leeds are said to be considering making an official complaint to UEFA after Spartak officials claim they were offered money by the Yorkshire club to play both legs of the tie in England... David O'Leary publicly sings the praises of his young side going into the UEFA encounter with Spartak, saying that they have performed well beyond the call of duty both in Europe and in the Premiership... O'Leary describes how he faced Spartak Moscow 18 years ago with Arsenal, saying they were one of the toughest sides he ever faced in his playing career – The Gunners were crushed 8-4 in 1981 by a Spartak team who were captained by current coach Romantsev... The stakes are increased for Spartak players when Russia's deputy prime minister and loyal Spartak fan, Alexander Shokin, says it is the players' duty to match the mood of the Russian people – which he believes is on a high after military success in Chechnya – by beating Leeds.

PREMIERSHIP: Manchester United win the World Club Cup by beating Palmeiras of Brazil 1-0 in Tokyo... **Thierry Henry** says he is in paradise at Highbury after some sections of the media insist he is finding life difficult in England... **Steffen Iversen** has admitted he would like to sign a new, long-term deal at White Hart Lane... **Craig Burley** is sold by Celtic to Derby for £3 million, a move that angers his followers at Celtic... **Paolo di Canio** says West Ham team-mate **Joe Cole** is the best young talent he has seen in Britain or Italy.

THE FINAL SCORE!

DECEMBER 4		
Aston Villa	0-1	Newcastle
Bradford	1-1	Middlesbrough
Leicester	0-3	Arsenal
Man. United	5-1	Everton
Southampton	0-0	Coventry
Sunderland	4-1	Chelsea
Wimbledon	5-0	Watford

TOP OF THE PREMIERSHIP

	P	W	D	L	Pts
1. Man. United	16	11	3	2	36
2. Arsenal	17	11	2	4	35
3. Leeds	16	11	2	3	35
4. Sunderland	17	10	4	3	34

Derby County (0) 0
Leeds United (0) 1

Competition: FA Carling Premiership

Date: Sunday December 5, 1999

Attendance: 29,455

Game 23

Referee: P Alcock (Halstead) 7

THE GAME: Leeds went back to the top of the Premiership with a dramatic late penalty from Ian Harte, plunging Derby deeper into relegation trouble. Harte condemned The Rams to their seventh home defeat of the season – the sort of form befitting a team struggling for Premiership survival. Although Leeds left it late, they were a class above Jim Smith's side and only poor finishing prevented them from having the points in the bag by half time. United were in control for the entire game but could have paid a heavy price for failing to convert possession into goals after the break, when Nigel Martyn was forced to save well from Georgi Kinkladze and Steve Elliott.

LEEDS GOAL: Harte (penalty 90 mins): Kewell made a fine surging run into the area but was caught by Derby defender Carbonari. Harte convincingly beat the 'keeper from the spot.

MATCH RATING ★★★ LEAGUE POSITION: 1st

"They are realistic title contenders. The run they've been on is fantastic and they've got a great chance of going all the way." JIM SMITH, DERBY MANAGER

DERBY COUNTY		LEEDS UNITED	
Poom	6	Martyn	6
Carbonari	6	Kelly	6
Powell	7	Booked: 20 mins (foul)	
Johnson	5	Harte	6
Booked: 24 mins (foul)		Goal: 90 mins	
Sturridge	6	Radebe	7
Burton	6	Woodgate	6
Subbed: 81 mins (Christie)		Bridges	6
Delap	7	Kewell	8
Laursen	7	Bowyer	7
Booked: 60 mins (foul); Subbed 64 mins (Prior)		Huckerby	5
Elliott	8	Subbed: 77 mins (Smith)	
Kinkladze	7	McPhail	6
Subbed: 75 mins (Dorigo)		Subbed: 83 mins (Jones)	
Burley	5	Bakke	6
sub: Prior	6	Booked: 12 mins (foul)	
Booked: 90 mins (foul)		sub: Smith	
sub: Dorigo		Booked: 88 mins (foul)	
sub: Christie		sub: Jones	
Subs not used: Hoult, Nimni		Subs not used: Robinson, Mills, Duberry	

MATCH FACTS
Shots On Target
Derby 5-5 Leeds
Shots Off Target
Derby 1-12 Leeds
Hit Woodwork
Derby 0-1 Leeds
Corners
Derby 4-11 Leeds

HOW THEY LINED UP

Harry Kewell was too hot for the Derby defence to handle as Leeds ran The Rams ragged.

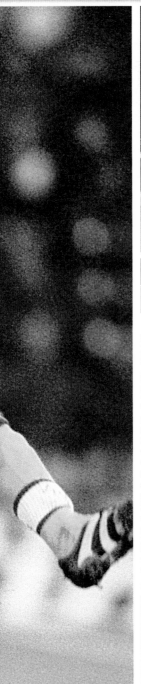

A goal from captain Lucas Radebe was enough to see Leeds through.

Leeds United (0) 1
Spartak Moscow (0) 0

2-2 on aggregate – Leeds win on away goals.

Competition: **UEFA Cup 3rd Rd 2nd Leg**

Date: **Thursday December 9, 1999**

Attendance: **39,732**

Referee: **A Lopez** (Spain) 6

Game 24

THE GAME: Lucas Radebe headed his team into the last 16 of the UEFA Cup as Leeds finally beat Spartak Moscow just six minutes from full-time in an epic encounter at Elland Road. Despite losing the first leg of the tie 2-1, United went through to the fourth round of the competition on the away goals rule, with Harry Kewell's strike in Sofia proving priceless. Substitute Spartak goalkeeper Andrei Smetanin made a string of superb saves for the Russian side to frustrate the Elland Road crowd, and it looked like the crucial goal would never come. But with less than 20 minutes to go, David O'Leary brought Huckerby on for Smith to vary United's attack and Radebe managed to grab the winner despite Spartak's consistent pressure.

LEEDS GOAL: Radebe *(84 mins):* McPhail sent a teasing corner into the box and Radebe popped up in a congested goalmouth to head only the third goal of his Leeds career.

MATCH RATING ★★★★ LEAGUE POSITION: 1st

> "We won't rest on our laurels, that's for certain. Being two points clear at the top of the league doesn't give you any right to do well in Europe." DAVID O'LEARY.

MATCH FACTS	
Shots On Target	
Leeds 8-7 Spartak	
Shots Off Target	
Leeds 15-15 Spartak	
Hit Woodwork	
Leeds 0-0 Spartak	
Corners	
Leeds 7-7 Spartak	

HOW THEY LINED UP

Leeds:
Martyn
Kelly — Radebe — Woodgate — Harte
Bakke — McPhail — Bowyer — Kewell
Smith — Bridges

Spartak:
Robson — Schirko
Tikhonov — Titov — Bulatov — Baranov
Evseev — Khlestov — Bouschmanov — Parfionov
Filimonov

LEEDS UNITED	
Martyn	7
Kelly	7
Woodgate	8
Radebe ⊕	7
Goal: 84 mins	
Harte	6
Bakke ☆	9
Bowyer	7
McPhail	7
Kewell	6
Smith ▢	6
Booked: 6 mins (foul); Subbed: 72 mins (Huckerby)	
Bridges	7
sub: Huckerby	

Subs not used: Haaland, Robinson, Mills, Jones, Hiden, Duberry.

SPARTAK MOSCOW	
Filimonov	6
Subbed: 38 mins (Smetanin)	
Parfionov ▢	7
Booked: 56 mins (unsporting behaviour)	
Khlestov	7
Bouschmanov ▢	7
Booked: 55 mins (unsporting behaviour)	
Bulatov ▢	8
Booked: 69 mins (foul)	
Evseev	7
Baranov	6
Titov	7
Tikhonov	6
Robson	6
Schirko	7
sub: Smetanin ☆	9

Subs not used: Ananko, Kechinov, Everton, Melyoshin, Mor, Bezrodny.

51

	Leeds United	(0) **2**
	Port Vale	(0) **0**

Competition: FA Cup 3rd Rd

Date: Sunday December 12, 1999

Attendance: 11,912

Referee: S Dunn (Bristol) 6

Game 25

THE GAME: Norway's Under-21 international Eirik Bakke, playing in his first ever FA Cup game, blasted Leeds through to a fourth round tie against Manchester City at Maine Road. Bakke, a £1.75 million capture from Sogndal in the summer, was only playing because David Batty hadn't recovered from a troublesome calf injury. But the Norwegian star filled Batty's shoes admirably, scoring twice in eight minutes in the second half at Elland Road. First Division strugglers Port Vale started well against David O'Leary's Premiership leaders, packing their midfield and closing Leeds down well. But Bakke put in a commanding performance and he showed his class when United stepped up a gear after the break. The crowd of just under 12,000 was disappointing, but with a packed series of Christmas fixtures approaching, including the next stage of the UEFA Cup, Leeds were just happy to be safely through to the next round of the competition without needing a replay.

LEEDS GOALS: Bakke (61 mins): Harte's cross was headed goalwards by Kelly, but Vale 'keeper Musselwhite could only punch the ball out to the corner of the penalty box – where Bakke finished powerfully for his first goal for his new club; **Bakke** (68 mins): Harte again provided the assist for the goal with a corner to the near post, where Bakke was on hand to flick the ball into the net from close range.

MATCH RATING ★★ LEAGUE POSITION: 1st

LEEDS UNITED		PORT VALE	
Martyn	6	Musselwhite ☆	8
Kelly	6	Gardner	7
Woodgate	7	Snijders ▫	6
Radebe	6	*Booked: 32 mins (foul)*	
Harte	7	Burns	7
Bowyer	6	Briscoe ▫	6
Subbed: 75 mins (Bridges)		*Booked: 74 mins (foul)*	
Bakke ⚽⚽ ☆	8	Eyre ▫	6
Goals: 61, 68 mins		*Booked: 71 mins (foul)*	
McPhail	6	Widdrington ▫	7
Kewell	6	*Booked: 60 mins (foul)*	
Smith ▫	6	Minton	6
Booked: 30 mins (foul); Subbed: 72 mins (Jones)		Tankard	6
		Subbed: 67 mins (Naylor)	
Huckerby	5	Foyle	5
sub: Jones	6	Rougier	7
sub: Bridges	6	*sub:* Naylor	6

Subs not used: Duberry, Mills, Robinson. | *Subs not used: Pilkington, Butler, Corden, Bogie.*

MATCH FACTS
Shots On Target
Leeds 6-1 Port Vale
Shots Off Target
Leeds 7-6 Port Vale
Hit Woodwork
Leeds 1-0 Port Vale
Corners
Leeds 12-2 Port Vale

HOW THEY LINED UP

Leeds:
Martyn
Kelly Woodgate Radebe Harte
Bowyer Bakke McPhail Kewell
Smith Huckerby

Port Vale:
Foyle Rougier
Minton Widdrington Briscoe Eyre
Tankard Gardner Snijders Burns
Musselwhite

Darren Huckerby got a rare start against Port Vale.

It was a devastating blow to go out of the Worthington Cup on penalties.

THIS WEEK...

IN THE NEWS

LEEDS UNITED: Young Norwegian midfielder **Eirik Bakke** earns rave reviews in the press after scoring his first two Leeds goals during an outstanding individual performance against Port Vale in the FA Cup... Leeds chief David O'Leary is the latest Premiership manager to be linked with a big-money move for the highly-rated Fulham striker **Geoff Horsfield**... United discover they will meet Italian giants Roma in the quarter-finals of the UEFA Cup, with the first leg to be played at Elland Road on March 2. Roma knocked Leeds out of the UEFA Cup in the 1998-99 season.

PREMIERSHIP: A lottery-winning Leicester City supporter decides to name his new racehorse after Turkey's midfield dynamo **Muzzy Izzet**... Arsenal and Man. United are said to be leading the chase to sign Japanese star **Shinji Ono**, the most highly-rated player in Asia... Everton have made their final contract offer to **Don Hutchison**, whose agent says AC Milan are among the clubs interested in the Scottish international's signature... West Ham value **Rio Ferdinand** at £15 million after Gerard Houllier shows an interest in taking the England defender to Anfield... Middlesbrough veteran **Gary Pallister** emerges as a target for the North American Soccer League, just weeks after clubs from America began showing an interest in his team-mate **Paul Gascoigne**...Southampton boss Dave Jones says that he hasn't received any offers for **Matthew Le Tissier**, apart from a cheeky enquiry from Conference side Woking... Derby boss Jim Smith has been told he is wasting his time with a £3.5 million bid for Bolton's talented young striker **Eidur Gudjohnsen**.

Leicester City (0) 0

Leeds United (0) 0

Leicester win 4-2 on penalties AET.

Competition: **Worthington Cup 4th Rd**

Date: **Wednesday December 15, 1999**

Attendance: **16,125**

Referee: **G Barber** (Tring) 6

Game 26

THE GAME: Leeds United suffered penalty heartbreak for the second year running against Leicester in the Worthington Cup at Filbert Street. Last season, a last-gasp Leicester spot-kick from Garry Parker knocked Leeds out of the Worthington Cup and on Wednesday night, The Foxes ended United's assault on four different trophies this season. The Yorkshire club lost 4-2 in a dramatic penalty shoot-out after the two sides could not be separated despite playing for 90 minutes and a further half an hour of extra time. Midfield ace Muzzy Izzet, who had scored a stunning equaliser in last year's fourth round clash, slotted home the crucial penalty that ended a disappointing night of football for United. Leeds played the entire extra-time period without inspirational skipper Lucas Radebe, who was handed a second yellow card in injury-time at the end of 90 minutes for a challenge on Leicester frontman Emile Heskey. David Batty was injured after just 20 minutes and he remains a concern for Leeds with some crucial games coming up.

MATCH RATING ★★★ **LEAGUE POSITION:** 2nd

LEICESTER CITY

Flowers	7
Taggart	7
Booked: 117 mins (foul)	
Walsh	6
Booked: 18 mins (foul)	
Izzet	6
Lennon	6
Subbed: 15 mins (Zagorakis)	
Heskey ☆	8
Booked: 29 mins (dissent)	
Savage	7
Elliott	7
Impey	7
Cottee	6
Subbed: 91 mins (Gunnlaugsson)	
Marshall	7
sub: *Zagorakis*	7
sub: *Gunnlaugsson*	

Subs not used: Arphexad, Gilchrist, Campbell.

LEEDS UNITED

Martyn	7
Kelly	7
Harte	6
Radebe	6
Booked: 28 mins (foul); Sent-off 90 mins (second bookable offence: foul)	
Woodgate	7
Bridges	6
Booked: 25 mins (foul); Subbed: 90 mins (Duberry)	
Kewell ☆	8
Bowyer	6
Booked: 59 mins (foul)	
McPhail	7
Bakke	7
Batty	6
Subbed: 20 mins (Jones)	
sub: *Jones*	7
sub: *Duberry*	

Subs not used: Huckerby, Robinson, Mills.

MATCH FACTS

Shots On Target
Leicester 8-4 Leeds

Shots Off Target
Leicester 8-3 Leeds

Hit Woodwork
Leicester 0-0 Leeds

Corners
Leicester 4-13 Leeds

HOW THEY LINED UP

Flowers

Walsh Elliott Taggart

Impey Izzet Lennon Savage

Cottee Marshall Heskey

Kewell Bridges

McPhail Bakke Batty Bowyer

Harte Radebe Woodgate Kelly

Martyn

THE FINAL SCORE!

DECEMBER 18

Arsenal	1-1	Wimbledon
Aston Villa	2-1	Sheff. Wed.
Bradford	2-0	Newcastle
Leicester	0-1	Derby
Liverpool	2-0	Coventry
Middlesbrough	2-1	Tottenham
Sunderland	2-0	Southampton
Watford	1-3	Everton
West Ham	2-4	Man. United

TOP OF THE PREMIERSHIP

	P	W	D	L	Pts
1. Man. United	17	12	3	2	39
2. Leeds	17	12	2	3	38
3. Sunderland	18	11	4	3	37
4. Arsenal	18	11	3	4	36

Leeds put in another towering performance to beat Chelsea 2-0 at Stamford Bridge.

 Chelsea (0) **0**

 Leeds United (0) **2**

 Game 27

Competition: **FA Carling Premiership**

Date: **Sunday December 19, 1999**

Attendance: **35,106**

Referee: **J Winter** (Stockton) 6

THE GAME: Stephen McPhail's first goals for the club sent Leeds back to the top of the Premiership. The 19-year-old midfielder drove home what was only Leeds' second shot on target following a spell of unrelenting Chelsea pressure at Stamford Bridge. The Blues had most of the possession, but their attempts to get back into the game were not helped by Frank Leboeuf's second-half dismissal with the score at 1-0.

LEEDS GOALS: McPhail *(66 mins):* Bowyer's cross from the right was missed by the Chelsea defence, allowing McPhail to shoot past a sprawling de Goey; **McPhail** *(88 mins):* A floated free-kick from McPhail on the right-wing bobbled through the legs of both Bakke and Poyet and into the Chelsea goal.

MATCH RATING ★★★★ LEAGUE POSITION: 1st

> "They probably felt they couldn't afford to wait, so they've bought success and built from there. We have taken the other route, but only because our young players are good enough." EDDIE GRAY, LEEDS ASSISTANT MANAGER

CHELSEA

de Goey	6
Leboeuf	4
Booked: 62 mins (foul); Sent-off: 69 mins (second bookable offence: foul)	
Desailly	6
Subbed: 46 mins (Hogh)	
Deschamps	6
Poyet	7
Sutton	5
Wise	7
Booked: 69 mins (foul)	
Di Matteo	5
Booked: 90 mins (foul)	
Ferrer	7
Flo	6
Subbed: 58 mins (Zola)	
Harley ☆	8
sub: Hogh	6
Subbed: 65 mins (Petrescu)	
sub: Zola	6
sub: Petrescu	6
Subs not used: Morris, Cudicini.	

LEEDS UNITED

Martyn	7
Kelly	7
Booked: 69 mins (foul)	
Harte	7
Booked: 52 mins (foul)	
Radebe	7
Woodgate	7
Bridges	6
Subbed: 49 mins (Wilcox)	
Kewell	6
Bowyer	7
Booked: 2 mins (foul); Subbed: 85 mins (Jones)	
Huckerby	7
McPhail ⊕ ⊕ ☆	8
Goals: 66 mins, 88 mins	
Bakke	7
sub: Wilcox	6
sub: Jones	
Subs not used: Robinson, Mills, Duberry.	

MATCH FACTS

Shots On Target
Chelsea 13-4 Leeds

Shots Off Target
Chelsea 9-3 Leeds

Hit Woodwork
Chelsea 0-1 Leeds

Corners
Chelsea 10-6 Leeds

HOW THEY LINED UP

```
                    de Goey

    Ferrer   Desailly   Leboeuf   Harley

  Di Matteo  Deschamps   Wise    Poyet

               Flo    Sutton

          Bridges    Huckerby

    Kewell  McPhail   Bakke   Bowyer

    Harte  Woodgate  Radebe   Kelly

                   Martyn
```

THIS WEEK...

IN THE NEWS

LEEDS UNITED: Chelsea manager Gianluca Vialli has nothing except praise for Leeds after their 2-0 win at Stamford Bridge, saying: "They kept calm, they waited and then scored"... United sign Blackburn winger and former England star **Jason Wilcox** for £3 million in a move that could release **Harry Kewell** to play in a more attacking role alongside **Michael Bridges**. Wilcox is keen to play Premiership football again and he has the added incentive of playing his way into the England squad, which is lacking quality left-footed players.

PREMIERSHIP: A book by 'The Daily Telegraph' football journalist Mihir Bose claims that there are political problems in the upper echelons of Manchester United Football Club with chairman Martin Edwards and Sir Alex Ferguson repeatedly clashing over financial matters... Wimbledon's new Norwegian owners admit that they are in serious financial trouble and are struggling to pay the second half of **John Hartson's** £7 million transfer fee, which is due to be paid to West Ham in the near future... In his programme notes, Chelsea chairman Ken Bates tells **Jody Morris** to put a stop to eating hamburgers and forget about flash cars and nightclubs... Sunderland striker **Niall Quinn** reveals he broke his nose for the 13th time during the FA Cup tie against Portsmouth... Ex-England coach Glenn Hoddle, already linked with the Portsmouth job, has now been mentioned as a potential replacement for John Gregory at Aston Villa... Blackburn's **Ashley Ward** could be the man to solve Spurs' goalscoring problems.

THE FINAL SCORE!

DECEMBER 19

Chelsea 0-2 Leeds

TOP OF THE PREMIERSHIP

	P	W	D	L	Pts
1. Leeds	18	13	2	3	41
2. Man. United	17	12	3	2	39
3. Sunderland	18	11	4	3	37
4. Arsenal	18	11	3	4	36

Leeds United (2) 2
Leicester City (1) 1

 Game 28

Competition: **FA Carling Premiership**

Date: **Sunday December 26, 1999**

Attendance: **40,105**

Referee: **M Halsey** (Welwyn) 6

THE GAME: Leeds gained revenge for their Worthington Cup exit with a convincing display at Elland Road. Despite falling behind after just ten minutes, Leeds dominated the game and had several chances saved by Pegguy Arphexad in Leicester's goal. Emile Heskey had a miserable afternoon up front – he was well marked by the Leeds defence and could not add to Tony Cottee's early strike. United fans were just glad that two goals in the first half meant they had finally beaten The Foxes.

LEEDS GOALS: Bridges *(29 mins):* Kewell whipped in a low cross from the right and Bowyer dummied, leaving Bridges to slot home from the edge of the Leicester area; **Bowyer** *(45 mins):* Bridges curled a pass into the box and Bowyer jinked past his marker to pick his spot in the top corner of the goal.
LEICESTER GOAL: Cottee *(10 mins):* Leeds defender Kelly was caught trying to dribble his way out of trouble, allowing Oakes to clip in a cross which Cottee met at the near post.

MATCH RATING ★★★★ LEAGUE POSITION: 1st

"Harry Kewell is an outstanding player. Leeds lead the league and deservedly so – there's no reason why they shouldn't continue to do so." MARTIN O'NEILL, LEICESTER CITY MANAGER

LEEDS UNITED		LEICESTER CITY	
Martyn	6	Arphexad	☆8
Booked: 16 mins (foul)		Elliott	6
Kelly	5	Taggart	6
Radebe	7	Gilchrist	6
Woodgate	7	*Subbed: 65 mins (Zagorakis)*	
Harte	6	Sinclair	6
Bowyer	7	Savage	6
Goal: 45 mins		Izzet	7
Bakke	7	Eadie	7
McPhail	7	Oakes	6
Kewell	☆8	Cottee	7
Bridges	6	*Goal: 10 mins*	
Booked: 25 mins (foul); Goal: 29 mins		Heskey	5
Huckerby	6	*sub: Zagorakis*	6
Subbed: 77 mins (Wilcox)		*Booked: 82 mins (foul)*	
sub: Wilcox		**Subs not used:** Gunnlaugsson, Campbell, Thomas, Hodges.	
Booked: 79 mins (foul)			

Subs not used: Mills, Jones, Duberry, Robinson.

MATCH FACTS
Shots On Target
Leeds 12-2 Leicester
Shots Off Target
Leeds 7-3 Leicester
Hit Woodwork
Leeds 2-0 Leicester
Corners
Leeds 13-4 Leicester

HOW THEY LINED UP
Martyn
Kelly Woodgate Radebe Harte
Bowyer Bakke McPhail Kewell
Bridges Huckerby
Heskey Cottee
Savage Eadie Izzet Oakes Gilchrist
Taggart Sinclair Elliott
Arphexad

Kewell's fine performance in the 2-1 win over Leicester rightly impressed Foxes manager Martin O'Neill.

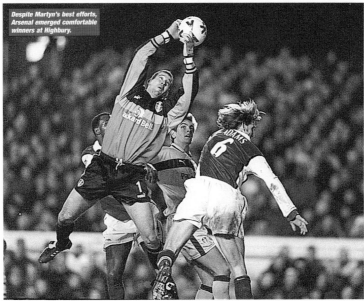

Despite Martyn's best efforts, Arsenal emerged comfortable winners at Highbury.

Arsenal (1) 2
Leeds United (0) 0

Competition: FA Carling Premiership

Date: Tuesday December 28, 1999

Attendance: 38,096

Referee: G Poll (Tring) 6

Game 29

THE GAME: After Arsenal's defeat to Coventry on Boxing Day, Arsene Wenger's side desperately needed to take three points from the game against the table-topping Yorkshiremen. Leeds arrived at Highbury in fine form but were brought down to earth by a makeshift Arsenal team that was short of key players in defence. The Gunners were still able to neutralise United's attacking threat, though. They struck first through Freddie Ljungberg and rarely looked troubled as the first half ended 1-0. Unfortunately for Leeds supporters, it was the same story after the break, with Arsenal looking more likely to double their lead than United were of grabbing an equaliser. The game was effectively over when Thierry Henry blasted in to make it 2-0 after constant pressure on the Leeds defence.

ARSENAL GOALS: Ljungberg *(31 mins):* Kanu shot from the edge of the area, only for Martyn to parry directly into the path of Ljungberg, who netted from five yards; **Henry** *(59 mins):* Kanu played an exquisite pass to Henry who brilliantly turned his marker to shoot low and powerfully past Martyn.

MATCH RATING ★★★★ LEAGUE POSITION: 1st

MATCH FACTS

Shots On Target
Arsenal 11-2 Leeds

Shots Off Target
Arsenal 10-2 Leeds

Hit Woodwork
Arsenal 0-0 Leeds

Corners
Arsenal 9-3 Leeds

HOW THEY LINED UP

Seaman

Luzhny Adams Grimandi Silvinho

Ljungberg Petit Vieira Overmars

Kanu Henry

Smith Bridges

Kewell McPhail Bakke Bowyer

Harte Radebe Woodgate Kelly

Martyn

ARSENAL

Seaman	7
Vieira	8
Adams	7
Ljungberg	7

Goal: 31 mins; Booked: 64 mins (foul)

Overmars	☆ 8

Booked: 65 mins (foul)

Henry	7

Goal: 59 mins; Subbed: 74 mins (Suker)

Silvinho	6
Petit	6

Subbed: 88 mins (Winterburn)

Grimandi	7
Luzhny	7
Kanu	6

Booked: 66 mins (dissent)

sub: Suker

sub: Winterburn

Subs not used: Dixon, Barrett, Manninger.

LEEDS UNITED

Martyn	☆ 8
Kelly	6

Booked: 76 mins (foul)

Harte	7
Radebe	7
Woodgate	6
Bridges	6

Booked: 51 mins (dissent)

Kewell	7

Booked: 38 mins (dissent)

Bowyer	8

Subbed: 80 mins (Jones)

McPhail	6
Smith	5

Booked: 36 mins (foul); Subbed: 80 mins (Wilcox)

Bakke	6

sub: Jones

sub: Wilcox

Subs not used: Robinson, Duberry, Mills.

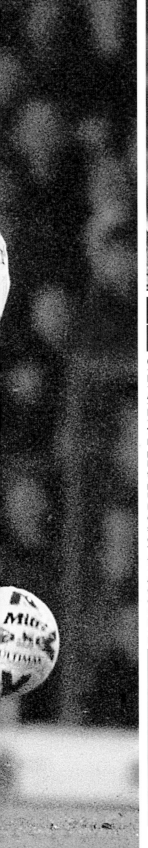

JANUARY

"We have a great belief in the squad here. If the team keeps winning you never know what might happen – we have got to keep up with Man. United and Arsenal." Darren Huckerby

AFTER A HECTIC DECEMBER WHICH SAW LEEDS IN ACTION IN THE Worthington Cup, FA Cup, UEFA Cup and Premiership, the team began the new millennium with a far less hectic fixture schedule. Having been knocked out of the Worthington Cup by Leicester City, and with the next round of the UEFA Cup in March, it was time for The Whites to focus their attention on the Premiership and look forward to a good run in the FA Cup.

In the absence of David Batty, Norwegian youngster Eirik Bakke continued to be a revelation in the centre of the midfield with some truly outstanding displays. The latest news on the influential Batty was encouraging, though. Specialists in France, who had been treating his injury, said he wasn't far from a return to the first team, which was great news for the Leeds faithful.

With title favourites Manchester United heading off to Brazil for the Club World Championships, it gave David O'Leary's side the perfect chance to create a gap between themselves and the Premiership champions and build a psychological advantage in the race for the title. But somebody wasn't reading the script in January. The new millennium started with a 2-1 defeat at home to Aston Villa, with United continuing their poor run of form against The Villans in recent years. The fourth round of the FA Cup saw a return to winning ways though, as O'Leary's young charges destroyed Division One title-chasers Manchester City 5-2 at Maine Road.

Next up were Sunderland in the Premiership, where Leeds gained three more vital points in a 2-1 win. The critics continued to dismiss United's title aspirations, but they were top of the table and the championship race was still wide open. Meanwhile, the media continued to link a galaxy of strikers with a move to Elland Road, with PSV Eindhoven's Ruud van Nistelrooy and Chelsea's Chris Sutton rumoured to be top of David O'Leary's shopping list.

THE GAMES

Jan. 3 v **Aston Villa** (h)

Jan. 9 v **Man. City** (a)

Jan. 23 v **Sunderland** (a)

Jan. 30 v **Aston Villa** (a)

TRANSFERS IN

None

TRANSFERS OUT

None

MATCH facts

Matchman Of The Month

GARY KELLY
Average Rating: 7.50

Leeds United   (0) **1**
Aston Villa   (1) **2**

Competition: **FA Carling Premiership**

Date: **Monday January 3, 2000**

Attendance: **40,027**

Referee: **U Rennie** (Sheffield) 5

Game 30

THE GAME: Manchester United were handed a New Year boost when table-topping Leeds slipped up against Aston Villa, who have now gone four games undefeated. If Leeds give many more performances like this they won't give the champions much of a challenge this year as they slumped to their second successive Premiership defeat. Only a magical goal from Harry Kewell and two brilliant saves by Nigel Martyn brightened up an otherwise dismal afternoon for Leeds. The most memorable thing about this Premiership game was the fact that Gareth Southgate found the net not once, but twice.

LEEDS GOAL: Kewell (46 mins): Controlled the ball on his chest while 35 yards out on the left-wing and caught everyone by surprise by unleashing a rocket shot into the far corner.

ASTON VILLA GOALS: Southgate (19 mins): Merson sent a teasing corner from the right which Southgate managed to hook towards goal. His first attempt was blocked but he was quick to stab the rebound past Martyn; **Southgate** (62 mins): Leeds conceded a free-kick on the edge of the penalty area and Merson arched the ball over to Southgate, who was given far too much room to head the ball back past Martyn and into the bottom left-hand corner of the Leeds goal.

MATCH RATING: ★★★ **LEAGUE POSITION:** 1st

LEEDS UNITED		ASTON VILLA	
Martyn	7	James	6
Kelly	6	Ehiogu	7
Duberry ▢	6	Southgate ⊕⊕	☆ 9
Booked: 16 mins (foul)		*Goals: 19, 62 mins*	
Woodgate	7	Barry	7
Harte ▢	6	Watson ▢	7
Booked: 85 mins (foul)		*Booked: 81 mins (foul)*	
Jones	6	Merson ▢	7
Subbed: 76 mins (Wilcox)		*Booked: 33 mins (foul)*	
Bakke	6	Boateng ▢	6
Haaland	5	*Booked: 49 mins (foul)*	
Kewell ⊕	☆ 7	Stone	6
Goal: 46 mins		Wright	7
Smith	6	Joachim	6
Subbed: 76 mins (Huckerby)		Carbone ▢	6
Bridges	6	*Booked: 41 mins (foul); Subbed: 86 mins (Vassell)*	
sub: Huckerby		*sub: Vassell* ▢	
sub: Wilcox		*Booked: 90 mins (unsporting behaviour)*	
Subs not used: Hiden, Robinson, Mills.		*Subs not used: Draper, Ghrayib, Cutler, Calderwood.*	

MATCH FACTS	HOW THEY LINED UP
Shots On Target	
Leeds 3-7 Aston Villa	
Shots Off Target	
Leeds 4-8 Aston Villa	
Hit Woodwork	
Leeds 0-0 Aston Villa	
Corners	
Leeds 5-5 Aston Villa	

HOW THEY LINED UP

James
Watson   Ehiogu   Southgate   Barry   Wright
Stone   Boateng   Merson
Joachim   Carbone
Smith   Bridges
Kewell   Bakke   Haaland   Jones
Harte   Woodgate   Duberry   Kelly
Martyn

Unfortunately for City, Leeds were back to their best in the FA Cup.

Manchester City (2) 2
Leeds United (3) 5

Competition: FA Cup 4th Rd

Date: **Sunday January 9, 2000**

Attendance: **29,240**

Referee: **D Gallagher** (Banbury) 7

Game 31

THE GAME: Manchester City's Premiership aspirations were put into perspective after being outclassed by David O'Leary's side in this FA Cup fourth round tie. City had been hoping for an upset following United's stuttering league form, but they were given a footballing lesson by the Premiership's leaders. Leeds twice came back from a goal down to crush The Blues at Maine Road. Shaun Goater and Ian Bishop put Joe Royle's side ahead twice in the first half, but Jason Wilcox, making his first start for Leeds, was instrumental in United's recovery.

MAN. CITY GOALS: Goater (2 mins): Kennedy crossed to Horlock, who knocked the ball on for Goater to flick a header past Martyn; **Bishop** (11 mins): The veteran midfielder struck a swerving right-foot shot that left Martyn with no chance.

LEEDS GOALS: Bakke (8 mins): Harte rose to meet a cross from McPhail and Bakke got the final touch to bring United level; **Smith** (20 mins): A simple tap-in following a goalbound header from Harte; **Kewell** (41 mins): Wilcox crossed to Harry Kewell at the far post and the Aussie star tucked the ball away from two yards out; **Bowyer** (66 mins): Met Wilcox's fine pass before firing past Weaver from 15 yards out; **Kewell** (88 mins): Substitute Huckerby outpaced Whitley on a 50-yard run before slipping the ball inside for Kewell to score.

MATCH RATING: ★★★★ **LEAGUE POSITION: 1st**

MATCH FACTS

Shots On Target

Man. City 6-18 Leeds

Shots Off Target

Man. City 2-8 Leeds

Hit Woodwork

Man. City 0-1 Leeds

Corners

Man. City 4-15 Leeds

HOW THEY LINED UP

Weaver

Edghill Jobson Wiekens Granville

Grant Bishop Horlock Kennedy

Goater Dickov

Kewell Smith

Wilcox McPhail Bakke Bowyer

Harte Radebe Woodgate Kelly

Martyn

MANCHESTER CITY

Weaver	☆ 9
Edghill	5
Wiekens	6
Horlock ▯	5
Booked: 16 mins (foul)	
Goater ⊕	6
Goal: 2 mins	
Dickov	5
Bishop ⊕	6
Goal: 11 mins	
Grant	4
Subbed: 55 mins (Whitley, J)	
Kennedy	6
Jobson	5
Granville	5
Subbed: 67 mins (Peacock)	
sub: Whitley, J	5
sub: Peacock	5

Subs not used: Crooks, Wright, Tiatto.

LEEDS UNITED

Martyn	7
Kelly	8
Harte ⊕	9
Goal: 8 mins	
Radebe	8
Woodgate	7
Kewell ⊕⊕	8
Goals: 41, 88 mins	
Bowyer ⊕	☆ 9
Goal: 66 mins	
McPhail	8
Wilcox	8
Smith ⊕ ▯	7
Goal: 20 mins; Booked: 25 mins (foul); Subbed: 86 mins (Huckerby)	
Bakke	7
sub: Huckerby	

Subs not used: Robinson, Mills, Jones, Duberry.

IN THE NEWS

LEEDS UNITED: David Batty is close to a first team return after receiving treatment in France… **Alf-Inge Haaland**, pushed down the pecking order following the arrival of winger Jason Wilcox from Blackburn Rovers, is attracting the interest of Bolton… United have denied preparing a £5 million bid for Chelsea misfit **Chris Sutton** following George Weah's arrival.

PREMIERSHIP: Darren Anderton rejects an increased pay offer of £24,000 a week to stay at Spurs… Aston Villa frontman **Dion Dublin** suffers an horrific neck injury against Sheffield Wednesday. Experts say the injury nearly put him in a wheelchair for life… Sunderland's **Thomas Sorensen** has agreed a new deal at the club despite interest from Lazio.

THE FINAL SCORE!

JANUARY 3		
Derby	2-0	Watford
Everton	2-2	Leicester
Leeds	1-2	**Aston Villa**
Newcastle	2-2	West Ham
Sheff. Wed.	1-1	Arsenal
Southampton	1-0	Bradford
Tottenham	1-0	Liverpool
Wimbledon	1-0	Sunderland
JANUARY 4		
Coventry	2-2	Chelsea
JANUARY 8		
Bradford	1-1	Chelsea
JANUARY 12		
Chelsea	1-0	Tottenham
JANUARY 15		
Arsenal	4-1	Sunderland
Chelsea	1-1	Leicester
Coventry	2-0	Wimbledon
Everton	2-2	Tottenham
Middlesbrough	1-4	**Derby**
Sheff. Wed.	2-0	Bradford
Watford	2-3	**Liverpool**
West Ham	1-1	Aston Villa
JANUARY 16		
Newcastle	5-0	Southampton
JANUARY 22		
Aston Villa	0-0	Chelsea
Bradford	3-2	Watford
Derby	0-0	Coventry
Leicester	1-3	**West Ham**
Liverpool	0-0	Middlesbrough
Southampton	2-0	Everton
Tottenham	0-1	**Sheff. Wed.**
Wimbledon	2-0	Newcastle

TOP OF THE PREMIERSHIP

		P	W	D	L	Pts
1.	Leeds	21	14	2	5	44
2.	Man. United	19	13	4	2	43
3.	Arsenal	22	13	4	5	43
4.	Liverpool	23	12	5	6	41

Sunderland (0) 1
Leeds United (1) 2

Competition: FA Carling Premiership

Date: Sunday January 23, 2000

Attendance: 41,947

Game 32

Referee: P Jones (Loughborough) 7

THE GAME: Leeds briefly returned to the top of the league ahead of Manchester United with a well-deserved victory over Sunderland, ending their hiccup of two defeats in the last two league games. The first half was a dour affair, which was only brought to life by an impressive strike from Jason Wilcox. The game really opened up in the second half though, the finesse of United's youngsters being matched by Sunderland's graft. The home side clawed it back to 2-1 through Kevin Phillips, and showed their renowned fighting qualities by pressing for an equaliser, but Leeds simply refused to let their lead slip.

SUNDERLAND GOAL: Phillips *(52 mins):* Took his scoring tally to 20 for the season when he latched on to a Woodgate mistake to take the ball forward and crack home a right-foot drive across 'keeper Martyn from a narrow angle.

LEEDS GOALS: Wilcox *(24 mins):* A superb strike. Receiving the ball 30 yards from goal, Wilcox strode forward and hit an unstoppable left-foot drive from just outside the box, which left the 'keeper helpless; **Bridges** *(50 mins):* Took his tally to 14 for the season when he finished a delightful move to score against his old team-mates. Kewell, after a good run on the left, crossed from the edge of the Sunderland box and Bridges lost his defender to side-foot past Sorensen from close range.

MATCH RATING: ★★★ **LEAGUE POSITION: 1st**

SUNDERLAND		LEEDS UNITED	
Sorensen	7	Martyn	7
Williams	5	Kelly	☆ 9
Gray	6	Harte	6
Subbed: 46 mins (Holloway)		Woodgate	7
Butler, P	☆ 8	Bridges ⊕	7
Bould	7	*Goal: 50 mins; Subbed: 74 mins*	
Subbed: 76 mins (Craddock)		*(Huckerby)*	
McCann	7	Kewell	7
Rae	6	Bowyer	7
Phillips ⊕	7	McPhail	6
Goal: 52 mins		Wilcox ⊕	7
Kilbane	7	*Goal: 24 mins*	
Roy	6	Bakke ▭	7
Subbed: 63 mins (Reddy)		*Booked: 62 mins (foul)*	
Schwarz	7	Duberry	8
sub: Holloway	5	*sub: Huckerby*	
sub: Reddy	6	**Subs not used:** *Haaland, Robinson, Mills,*	
sub: Craddock		*Jones.*	
Subs not used: *Marriott, Oster.*			

MATCH FACTS

Shots On Target
Sunderland 5-4 Leeds

Shots Off Target
Sunderland 7-6 Leeds

Hit Woodwork
Sunderland 0-0 Leeds

Corners
Sunderland 5-5 Leeds

HOW THEY LINED UP

Sorensen

Williams — Bould — Butler — Gray

Kilbane — Schwarz — McCann — Rae — Roy

Phillips

Kewell — Bridges

Wilcox — Bowyer — Bakke — McPhail

Harte — Duberry — Woodgate — Kelly

Martyn

Jason Wilcox had no trouble making friends at his new club.

Aston Villa brought high-flying Leeds crashing down to earth.

Aston Villa (1) 3
Leeds United (2) 2

Competition: FA Cup 5th Rd

Date: Sunday January 30, 2000

Attendance: 30,026

Referee: **G P Barber** (Tring) 7

Game 33

THE GAME: Aston Villa took their unbeaten run to 11 games with a memorable FA Cup win over Leeds. United had a good start at Villa Park, though, twice taking the lead in the first half with goals from Ian Harte and Eirik Bakke. But an outstanding hat-trick from Benito Carbone sent Villa into the quarter-finals of the competition. Carbone, who has yet to find the net in the Premiership for The Villans, rose to the occasion with a superb individual performance and capped it off with a contender for the Goal Of The Season. United were shocked by the Italian striker's opportunism, and in the second half David O'Leary's men lost the poise which had helped them control the match in the first half. For Leeds supporters, another year of FA Cup dreams ended in a competition United last won in 1972.

ASTON VILLA GOALS: Carbone *(32 mins):* A free-kick from the left found Watson on the right and his header into the middle was collected by Carbone, who fired home a low, precise shot from 15 yards; **Carbone** *(58 mins):* An inspired moment from the Italian. Spotting Martyn drifting away from his near post, he placed the ball into the top left-hand corner from all of 40 yards; **Carbone** *(59 mins):* Merson chipped the ball forward and ran on to head the ball into the middle for Carbone to complete his hat-trick with a close range header.

LEEDS GOALS: Harte *(13 mins):* Ehiogu and Kewell both challenged for McPhail's corner and the ball bounced up to Harte, who rammed home a shot from the edge of the area; **Bakke** *(38 mins):* Scored with a flying header from McPhail's left-wing cross for his third FA Cup goal in three games.

MATCH RATING: ★★★★★ LEAGUE POSITION: 2nd

MATCH FACTS

Shots On Target
Aston Villa 7-3 Leeds

Shots Off Target
Aston Villa 2-1 Leeds

Hit Woodwork
Aston Villa 0-0 Leeds

Corners
Aston Villa 2-3 Leeds

HOW THEY LINED UP

James

Watson Ehiogu Southgate Barry Wright

Stone Boateng Merson

Joachim Carbone

Kewell Bridges

Wilcox McPhail Bakke Bowyer

Harte Duberry Woodgate Kelly

Martyn

ASTON VILLA

James	6
Watson □	6

Booked: 41 mins (foul); Subbed: 46 mins (Delaney)

Southgate	7
Ehiogu	7
Barry	7
Wright	6
Stone	6
Boateng	7
Merson	8

Subbed: 72 mins (Hendrie)

Joachim	6
Carbone ⚽⚽⚽	☆ 9

Booked 22mins (foul); Goals: 32, 58, 59 mins

sub: Delaney	6
sub: Hendrie	6

Subs not used: *Thompson, Cutler, Walker.*

LEEDS UNITED

Martyn	6
Kelly	6
Duberry	6

Subbed: 70 mins (Mills)

Woodgate	6
Harte ⚽	7

Goal: 13 mins

Bowyer □	6

Booked: 37 mins (foul)

Bakke ⚽	7

Goal: 38 mins; Subbed: 84 mins (Huckerby)

McPhail	☆ 8
Wilcox □	6

Booked: 87 mins (foul)

Bridges	6

Subbed: 70 mins (Smith)

Kewell	7
sub: Mills	6
sub: Smith	6
sub: Huckerby	6

Subs not used: *Robinson, Jones.*

FEBRUARY

"If people say we're going to fall apart we can just go out and play our football without worrying – it takes the pressure off. But if we play well we'll win." Harry Kewell

FEBRUARY WAS ALWAYS GOING TO BE A SEVERE TEST OF LEEDS' title credentials. A look at the fixture list for the month saw that as well as an away trip to Gerard Houllier's in-form Liverpool, The Whites also had to entertain Tottenham – led by former Leeds boss George Graham – before facing a mouthwatering clash with title rivals Manchester United. With an end of month trip to the unpredictable Middlesbrough, it looked like a far from easy month on paper, and so it proved.

Liverpool had recovered from their shaky start to the campaign to become one of the Premiership's most consistent teams and boasted the meanest defence in the division. They proved their calibre by beating David O'Leary's side 3-1 to take maximum points for the season against The Whites.

Next up were Tottenham, with George Graham returning to Elland Road as the opposition manager. The match lived up to expectations with both sets of players sensing what the game meant to their fans. In a highly-charged, bad-tempered affair, Leeds emerged victorious with a narrow 1-0 win to stay hot on the heels of their next opponents, Manchester United.

Unfortunately, the win over Spurs proved to be The Whites' only victory in February. Manchester United arrived at Elland Road without David Beckham in the side following a training ground bust-up with his boss Alex Ferguson on the Friday. Leeds fans hoped they could close the gap on their title rivals, but were disappointed at the final whistle. The Red Devils were fresh from the World Club Championships and Andy Cole's single goal was enough to do the double over Leeds in their quest for another Premiership title. A trip to Middlesbrough ended the month, and despite creating enough chances to win three or four games, The Whites couldn't break the deadlock and had to be content with a 0-0 draw and a solitary point at The Riverside.

THE GAMES

Feb. 5 v **Liverpool** (a)

Feb. 12 v **Tottenham** (h)

Feb. 20 v **Man. United** (h)

Feb. 26 v **Middlesbrough** (a)

TRANSFERS IN

None

TRANSFERS OUT

None

MATCH facts

Matchman Of The Month

HARRY KEWELL
Average Rating: 7.50

65

Liverpool	(1) 3
Leeds United	(0) 1

Competition: FA Carling Premiership

Date: Saturday February 5, 2000

Attendance: 44,793

Game 34

Referee: M Reed (Birmingham) 7

THE GAME: Liverpool brushed Leeds aside with three top quality strikes in a pulsating top-of-the-table clash. Young midfielder Steven Gerrard was Liverpool's star man, dictating the game from central midfield and causing United all sorts of problems. Leeds couldn't be faulted for their commitment but their efforts were to no avail as The Reds won comfortably at Anfield. It boosts Liverpool's confidence as they attempt to play their way into contention for a Champions league place, but United will have to improve on this display if they wish to seriously challenge for the Premiership title.

LIVERPOOL GOALS: Hamann (19 mins): Gerrard fed the ball to Hamann who shot from 25 yards, via a slight deflection, into the left-hand side of Martyn's goal; **Berger** (69 mins): Received the ball 35 yards out from Smicer and was given too much room before unleashing an unstoppable shot into the roof of the net; **Murphy** (90 mins): Picked the ball up deep in midfield and carried it forward before hitting a sweet volley from 20 yards which again left Martyn without a hope.

LEEDS GOAL: Bowyer (62 mins): Wilcox took off on a run down the left-wing and delivered an inch-perfect cross to the far post. Bowyer was storming in and flung himself in the air to meet the ball and head home from inside the six-yard box.

MATCH RATING: ★★★★ **LEAGUE POSITION: 2nd**

LIVERPOOL	
Westerveld	7
Matteo	8
Hyypia	8
Henchoz	7
Carragher	6
Berger ⊕	8
Goal: 69 mins	
Gerrard ▢	☆ 8
Booked: 33 mins (foul)	
Hamann ▢ ⊕	7
Booked: 15 mins (foul); Goal: 19 mins	
Smicer	7
Camara	6
Subbed: 71 mins (Murphy)	
Meijer	7
sub: Murphy ⊕	
Goal: 90 mins	

Subs not used: Newby, Heggem, Neilsen, Staunton.

LEEDS UNITED	
Martyn	6
Harte ▢	6
Booked: 45 mins (foul)	
Woodgate	5
Duberry ▢	6
Booked: 54 mins (foul)	
Kelly	5
Wilcox	7
Bowyer ⊕	7
Goal: 62 mins	
McPhail	6
Subbed: 75 mins (Huckerby)	
Bakke	5
Kewell	☆ 8
Smith ▢	5
Booked: 66 mins (foul); Subbed: 75 mins (Bridges)	
sub: Bridges	
sub: Huckerby	

Subs not used: Robinson, Mills, Jones.

MATCH FACTS	
Shots On Target	
Liverpool 5-3 Leeds	
Shots Off Target	
Liverpool 9-1 Leeds	
Hit Woodwork	
Liverpool 0-0 Leeds	
Corners	
Liverpool 8-3 Leeds	

HOW THEY LINED UP

Westerveld

Carragher Henchoz Hyypia Matteo

Smicer Gerrard Hamann Berger

Meijer Camara

Kewell Smith

Wilcox McPhail Bakke Bowyer

Harte Duberry Woodgate Kelly

Martyn

Though their effort couldn't be faulted, United just weren't good enough to beat Liverpool at Anfield.

The confrontations took the shine off this win to keep Leeds chasing top spot.

Leeds United (1) 1
Tottenham Hotspur (0) 0

Competition: FA Carling Premiership
Date: Saturday February 12, 2000
Attendance: 40,127
Referee: D Gallagher (Banbury) 5

Game 35

THE GAME: Harry Kewell's tenth goal of the season kept United's interest in the title race alive, securing a valuable win in an ill-tempered game with Tottenham at Elland Road. With Manchester United losing to Newcastle on the same day, this win set up a mouth-watering match between the Premiership's top two clubs next Sunday. The margin of victory would have been greater if Alan Smith had finished the opportunities that came his way, but this was a valuable three points that kept Leeds in touch at the top. The second half deteriorated into an ugly affair with some niggling challenges that caused some unnecessary confrontations between the two sides.

LEEDS GOAL: Kewell (23 mins): Duberry headed forward to Kewell, who nodded the ball over 'keeper Walker after he had sprinted out of his area. Kewell then cleverly cut inside Campbell before slotting the ball into the unguarded net.

MATCH RATING: ★★★ **LEAGUE POSITION:** 2nd

"It's not a ruthless streak that's missing, it's learning to put the ball away. I told Harry Kewell last season the thing I wanted most from him was goals." DAVID O'LEARY

MATCH FACTS
Shots On Target
Leeds 3-2 Tottenham
Shots Off Target
Leeds 7-6 Tottenham
Hit Woodwork
Leeds 0-0 Tottenham
Corners
Leeds 5-4 Tottenham

HOW THEY LINED UP

Martyn

Kelly Woodgate Duberry Harte

Jones Bakke Bowyer Wilcox

Smith Kewell

Korsten Armstrong

Ginola Sherwood Clemence Anderton

Taricco Campbell Perry Carr

Walker

LEEDS UNITED
Martyn	7
Kelly ▢	7
Booked: 71 mins (foul)	
Woodgate	7
Duberry	7
Harte	7
Bowyer ▢	6
Booked: 50 mins (foul)	
Bakke ▢	6
Booked: 58 mins (foul); Subbed: 85 mins (Haaland)	
Jones ▢	6
Booked: 90 mins (foul)	
Wilcox	6
Kewell ⊕	★8
Goal: 23 mins; Subbed: 68 mins (Huckerby)	
Smith	7
sub: Huckerby	6
sub: Haaland	

Subs not used: Mills, Maybury, Robinson.

TOTTENHAM HOTSPUR
Walker	6
Carr ▢	7
Booked: 63 mins (foul)	
Perry	6
Campbell	6
Taricco	6
Anderton ▢	6
Booked: 82 mins (foul)	
Sherwood ▢	★8
Booked: 40 mins (foul)	
Clemence ▢	6
Booked: 29 mins (foul); Subbed: 74 mins (Nielsen)	
Ginola	5
Subbed: 78 mins (Dominguez)	
Korsten	7
Armstrong ▢	5
Booked: 42 mins (foul)	
sub: Nielsen	
sub: Dominguez	

Subs not used: Scales, Young, Baardsen.

THIS WEEK...

IN THE NEWS

LEEDS UNITED: Referee Mike Reed is asked to report to the FA after he appeared to celebrate when Liverpool's Patrik Berger scored against Leeds... The blow of losing **Michael Bridges** through injury for the Tottenham game is softened by news that **David Batty** is on the verge of a return to the first team... Republic Of Ireland coach Mick McCarthy tips midfield ace **Stephen McPhail** to become an international star of the future. **PREMIERSHIP:** Sir Alex Ferguson criticises his players for their rash protests after conceding a penalty against Middlesbrough... Former England coach Glenn Hoddle takes over the reins at Southampton... Man. United finalise a four-year sponsorship deal with Vodafone worth £30 million... Chelsea's **Frank Leboeuf** has been handed a two match ban on top of the two game suspension that he received for stamping on **Harry Kewell** in Chelsea's 2-0 defeat by Leeds.

THE FINAL SCORE!

FEBRUARY 2		
Sheff. Wed.	0-1	**Man. United**

FEBRUARY 5		
Aston Villa	4-0	Watford
Bradford	2-1	Arsenal
Derby	3-3	Sheff. Wed.
Leicester	2-1	Middlesbrough
Liverpool	3-1	Leeds
Man. United	3-2	Coventry
Southampton	2-1	West Ham
Sunderland	2-2	Newcastle
Tottenham	0-1	**Chelsea**

FEBRUARY 6		
Wimbledon	0-3	**Everton**

FEBRUARY 12		
Chelsea	3-1	Wimbledon
Coventry	3-2	Sunderland
Everton	2-1	Derby
Leeds	1-0	Tottenham
Newcastle	3-0	Man. United
Sheff. Wed	0-1	**Southampton**
Watford	1-1	Leicester
West Ham	5-4	Bradford

TOP OF THE PREMIERSHIP
		P	W	D	L	Pts
1.	Man. United	23	16	5	2	53
2.	Leeds	23	15	2	6	47
3.	Arsenal	24	13	5	6	44
4.	Liverpool	24	11	7	6	40

67

Leeds United (0) 0
Manchester United (0) 1

Game 36

Competition: FA Carling Premiership

Date: Sunday February 20, 2000

Attendance: 40,160

Referee: P Jones (Loughborough) 8

THE GAME: Manchester United stretched the gap at the top of the table to six points after Andy Cole's deadly strike was enough to beat Leeds at Elland Road. Sir Alex Ferguson left out David Beckham after an alleged training ground incident, but the England star wasn't missed as Fergie's charges did a professional job, denying Leeds any space in the middle of the park. Lee Bowyer missed a gilt-edged chance to level the scoreline when he somehow put the ball over from just three yards out, and the home team hit the woodwork three times but just couldn't score. It clearly wasn't Leeds' day, and with only one win in four games and trailing The Red Devils by six points at the top of the league, pessimistic observers said this result marked the end of their 1999-2000 title hopes.

MANCHESTER UNITED GOAL: Cole (52 mins): Radebe failed to muscle Cole off the ball and as Martyn hesitated, the Man. United striker hooked the ball past the Leeds 'keeper.

MATCH RATING: ★★★ **LEAGUE POSITION: 2nd**

> "Any club that gets more points than Man. United will win the league. They've done it all before and they know what they've got to do to repeat it. United are still the best team in the country." LEEDS STRIKER DARREN HUCKERBY

LEEDS UNITED		MANCHESTER UNITED	
Martyn	7	Bosnich	8
Kelly	6	Neville, G	7
Radebe	6	Stam ☐	7
Woodgate	7	*Booked: 45 mins (foul)*	
Harte	7	Silvestre ☆	9
Bakke	7	Irwin ☐	7
Bowyer	5	*Booked: 20 mins (foul)*	
Jones ☐	7	Scholes	7
Booked: 90 mins (foul)		Keane	8
Wilcox	7	Butt	7
Smith	7	Giggs	6
Kewell ☐ ☆	8	Yorke	6
Booked: 62 mins (dissent)		*Subbed: 29 mins (Sheringham)*	
Subs not used: Haaland, Hopkin, Huckerby, Mills, Robinson.		Cole ⊕	8
		Goal: 52 mins	
		sub: Sheringham	7
		Subs not used: Neville, P, Cruyff, van der Gouw, Berg.	

MATCH FACTS			HOW THEY LINED UP
Shots On Target			
Leeds 7-3 Man. United			
Shots Off Target			
Leeds 5-6 Man. United			
Hit Woodwork			
Leeds 3-1 Man. United			
Corners			
Leeds 10-6 Man. United			

HOW THEY LINED UP

Martyn

Kelly — Radebe — Woodgate — Harte

Jones — Bakke — Bowyer — Wilcox

Smith — Kewell

Cole — Yorke

Giggs — Butt — Keane — Scholes

Irwin — Silvestre — Stam — Neville, G

Bosnich

kv digital

The champions stopped Kewell & co in their tracks at Elland Road.

Lee Bowyer just couldn't score in a frustrating 0-0 draw at The Riverside.

Middlesbrough (0) 0
Leeds United (0) 0

Game 37

Competition: FA Carling Premiership

Date: Saturday February 26, 2000

Attendance: 34,800

Referee: U Rennie (Sheffield) **6**

THE GAME: As goalless draws go, this was about as exciting as it gets. Neither side let up in a highly-charged encounter before a record crowd of 34,800 at The Riverside. The game was played at a cracking pace, with tremendous commitment from both teams. Leeds missed a host of chances to take all three points, having two goals disallowed which would have been enough to close the gap on Manchester United – who could only draw at Wimbledon. Lee Bowyer did everything except score, having a first-half effort ruled out for offside, before hitting the bar with a header and seeing another effort go agonisingly wide. Middlesbrough defender Gianluca Festa was sent-off for two fouls in two minutes at the end of the game but Boro hung on to earn a point. The result was seen as two points lost by David O'Leary's side, and was a major blow to their prospects of gaining ground on the champions and current leaders of the Premiership Manchester United.

MATCH RATING: ★★★★ LEAGUE POSITION: 2nd

> "At the end of the day, it's all about taking chances and today we just didn't take them." DAVID O'LEARY

MATCH FACTS

Shots On Target
Middlesbrough 5-13 Leeds

Shots Off Target
Middlesbrough 5-12 Leeds

Hit Woodwork
Middlesbrough 1-2 Leeds

Corners
Middlesbrough 2-4 Leeds

HOW THEY LINED UP

Schwarzer

Cooper · Pallister · Festa · Fleming

Summerbell · Maddison · Juninho · Ziege

Ricard · Campbell

Kewell · Smith

Wilcox · Bowyer · Haaland · Hopkin

Harte · Radebe · Woodgate · Mills

Martyn

MIDDLESBROUGH

Schwarzer	☆ 8
Fleming	7
Festa ▨▨	7
Booked: 84 mins (foul); Sent-off: 86 mins (second bookable offence: foul)	
Pallister ▨	7
Booked: 16 mins (foul)	
Cooper	7
Ziege ▨	6
Booked: 89 mins (foul)	
Juninho	7
Maddison	7
Subbed: 74 mins (Cummins)	
Summerbell	7
Campbell	6
Subbed: 74 mins (Armstrong)	
Ricard	6
Subbed: 87 mins (Vickers)	
sub: *Armstrong*	
sub: *Cummins*	
sub: *Vickers*	

Subs not used: Stockdale, Beresford.

LEEDS UNITED

Martyn	7
Mills ▨	6
Booked: 79 mins (foul)	
Woodgate	7
Radebe	7
Harte	7
Haaland ▨	☆ 8
Booked: 80 mins (foul)	
Hopkin	7
Subbed: 87 mins (Bridges)	
Bowyer	6
Wilcox	6
Smith	6
Subbed: 56 mins (Huckerby)	
Kewell ▨	6
Booked: 67 mins (foul)	
sub: *Bridges*	
sub: *Huckerby*	6

Subs not used: Duberry, Maybury, Robinson.

MARCH

"The target is the Champions League. We've got eight games left – four at home and four away. We'll try to win all of them. Let's see where they get us." David O'Leary

FOR A CAMPAIGN THAT PROMISED SO MUCH FOR SO LONG, LEEDS were in danger of finishing the season empty-handed. Having been knocked out of the FA Cup and Worthington Cup, and with their form in the league stuttering, The Whites needed to get back on track – and quickly. Despite hanging on to second place throughout March, Arsenal and Liverpool were in fine form and David O'Leary again emphasised that the most important thing was to qualify for the Champions League. After a two-month winter break in Europe, Leeds returned to UEFA Cup action for their biggest test to date – a fourth round tie against their conquerors in 1999, AS Roma.

The first leg in the Italian capital was a gritty defensive display from Leeds in the face of intense pressure, which saw them take a 0-0 scoreline back to Elland Road. All of the team were heroes, but none more so than goalkeeper Nigel Martyn, who pulled off some truly world-class saves to keep the tie goalless. The second leg at home in Leeds was yet another nail-biting affair, but a Harry Kewell strike was enough to put them into the quarter-finals.

Between the European games, United's league form picked up again, and despite the intensity and the importance of these matches, David O'Leary's youngsters continued to defy the odds. They crushed Coventry 3-0 at Elland Road and maintained their superiority in Yorkshire with a crucial 2-1 victory at Bradford. After losing to Wimbledon at Selhurst Park earlier in the season, revenge was sweet as The Dons were swept aside 4-1 at home.

The Whites went into the quarter-finals of the UEFA Cup with the uneasy label of being favourites to overcome Czech opponents Slavia Prague. But if the players were feeling the pressure, they didn't show it. The team gained a comprehensive 3-0 home win to make the second leg a formality, winning the tie 4-2 on aggregate. They were back on track and ready for anyone.

THE GAMES

March 2 v **AS Roma** (a)
March 5 v **Coventry** (h)
March 9 v **AS Roma** (h)
March 12 v **Bradford** (a)
March 16 v **Slavia Prague** (h)
March 19 v **Wimbledon** (h)
March 23 v **Slavia Prague** (a)
March 26 v **Leicester** (a)

TRANSFERS IN

Shaun Allaway
Position: **Goalkeeper**
Fee: **£300,000**
From: **Reading**

TRANSFERS OUT

None

MATCH facts
Matchman Of The Month

HARRY KEWELL
Average Rating: 8.00

A hug from the gaffer always makes young Alan feel treasured!

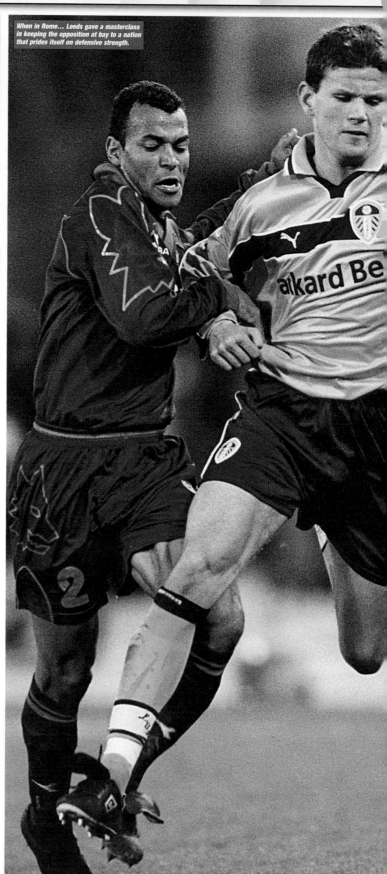
When in Rome... Leeds gave a masterclass in keeping the opposition at bay to a nation that prides itself on defensive strength.

FROM THE PAGES OF *MATCH*

As the season hurtled towards its climax, the 'experts' predicted that **LEEDS'** young stars would falter. **MATCH** asked **HARRY KEWELL** and **MICHAEL BRIDGES** how they were bearing up.

Do you really believe you won't win the title this year?
Bridges: "David O'Leary has told us all to take one game at a time and he says that to the newspapers as well. We have a ready-made excuse that we're too young, just in case we don't end up winning anything this year."
Kewell: "I'd say that we've got as good a chance as anyone in the league. All season there's only been one goal in our minds – that's winning the championship."

So do you think you'll be there or thereabouts at the end of the season?
Bridges: "I think we've got what it takes. It will come right down to the wire at the end of the season and I think we'll still be right up there challenging for the title."
Kewell: "We're in the league because we want to win it and I really believe we're capable of doing that. It's going to be close because there are some other good sides there who are in with a shout of winning it."

Do you think the UEFA Cup will become a distraction?
Kewell: "No, I think it's a good thing for us. Every game we have in Europe gives us more experience and that's got to be a good thing. We're getting to the latter stages of the competition and playing against the best teams in Europe, which will stand us in good stead for the coming year."

AS Roma (0) **0**
Leeds United (0) **0**

Competition: **UEFA Cup 4th Rd 1st leg**

Date: **Thursday March 2, 2000**

Attendance: **37,726**

Referee: **G Veissiere** (France) 6

Game 38

THE GAME: In an enthralling match at the Olympic Stadium, Leeds gave themselves a good chance of reaching the last eight of the UEFA Cup with a 0-0 draw in the Italian capital. Roma threw everything at United, with 23-year-old Francesco Totti involved in all of his side's best moments. But Leeds put in a disciplined defensive performance, with Lucas Radebe, Jonathan Woodgate and Nigel Martyn outstanding at the back in keeping Totti and company at bay. United did have chances of their own, with Bakke and Kewell squandering opportunities to score a crucial away goal, but the travelling fans and Leeds chief David O'Leary returned home happy with the result.

MATCH RATING: ★★★★ **LEAGUE POSITION:** 2nd

AS ROMA		LEEDS UNITED	
Antonioli	7	Martyn	☆ 8
Zago	7	Radebe	8
Aldair	7	*Booked: 62 mins (foul)*	
Mangone	7	Haaland	7
Cafu	7	Woodgate	8
Nakata	6	Jones	7
Tommasi	6	Kelly	7
Candela	8	Bakke	7
Totti	☆ 9	Bowyer	6
Delvecchio	7	Harte	7
Montella	7	Bridges	8
		Subbed: 71 mins (Smith)	
		Kewell	8
		sub: Smith	

Subs not used: Lupatelli, Di Francesco, Tomic, Gurenko, Rinaldi, Blasi, Pereira.

Subs not used: Robinson, Huckerby, Maybury, Mills, Duberry.

MATCH FACTS	
Shots On Target	
AS Roma 14-4 Leeds	
Shots Off Target	
AS Roma 10-6 Leeds	
Hit Woodwork	
AS Roma 0-0 Leeds	
Corners	
AS Roma 9-4 Leeds	

HOW THEY LINED UP

Antonioli

Cafu Aldair Mangone Zago Candela

Tommasi Nakata Totti

Montella Delvecchio

Bridges

Kewell Bowyer Haaland Bakke Jones

Harte Radebe Woodgate Kelly

Martyn

A good team performance earned United three points against visitors Coventry.

Leeds United (2) 3
Coventry City (0) 0

Competition: FA Carling Premiership

Date: Sunday March 5, 2000

Attendance: 38,710

Referee: J Winter (Stockton) 7

Game 39

THE GAME: Leeds ended a goal drought that had spanned three matches and 342 minutes as they gave The Sky Blues a lesson in football and closed the gap on leaders Manchester United down to four points. Harry Kewell was at his brilliant best, scoring the first goal after just five minutes and cleverly setting up the second for Michael Bridges to coolly round the stranded Coventry goalkeeper Hedman just before half-time. Five minutes from the end of a one-sided contest, substitute Darren Huckerby came on against his old club and laid on the third goal for the in-form Jason Wilcox. Coventry slipped to their third successive Premiership defeat and are still not yet safe from the relegation dogfight at the bottom of the table. For Leeds, the 3-0 win helped put their Premiership ambitions back on track after two league games without a win.

LEEDS GOALS: Kewell (5 mins): Burrows fouled Bridges just outside the right-hand edge of the penalty area. Harte tapped the ball square to Kewell and the Australian star hit a left-foot shot into the bottom left-hand corner of the net; **Bridges** (42 mins): Bakke's throughball was cleverly flicked on by Kewell to the unmarked Bridges. The striker raced into the penalty area, rounded 'keeper Hedman and shot into the open goal; **Wilcox** (85 mins): Substitute Huckerby had only been on the field five minutes when he raced away on the left and played the ball inside to Wilcox, who drove it past Hedman from ten yards.

MATCH RATING: ★★★ **LEAGUE POSITION: 2nd**

MATCH FACTS

Shots On Target
Leeds 5-4 Coventry

Shots Off Target
Leeds 11-5 Coventry

Hit Woodwork
Leeds 0-0 Coventry

Corners
Leeds 8-4 Coventry

LEEDS UNITED

Martyn	7
Kelly	7
Radebe	8
Woodgate	8
Subbed: 46 mins (Haaland)	
Harte	7
Bowyer	6
Subbed: 89 mins (Jones)	
Bakke	8
McPhail	8
Wilcox ⊙	8
Goal: 85 mins	
Bridges ⊙	8
Goal: 42 mins; Subbed: 80 mins (Huckerby)	
Kewell ⊙	☆9
Goal: 5 mins	
sub: Haaland	7
sub: Huckerby	
sub: Jones	

Subs not used: Smith, Robinson.

COVENTRY CITY

Hedman	6
Quinn	5
Subbed: 46 mins (Shaw)	
Hendry	7
Breen	6
Burrows	6
Chippo	6
Eustace	6
McAllister	☆8
Whelan	5
Roussel	6
Zuniga	5
Subbed: 60 mins (Normann)	
sub: Shaw	7
sub: Normann	6

Subs not used: Konjic, Pead, Hyldgaard.

HOW THEY LINED UP

Martyn

Kelly • Woodgate • Radebe • Harte

Bowyer • Bakke • McPhail • Wilcox

Bridges • Kewell

Roussel • Zuniga

Whelan • Eustace • McAllister • Chippo

Burrows • Breen • Hendry • Quinn

Hedman

 Leeds United (0) **1**

 AS Roma (0) **0**

Leeds win 1-0 on aggregate.

Competition: **UEFA Cup 4th Rd 2nd Leg**

Date: **Thursday March 9, 2000**

Attendance: **39,149**

Referee: **J-M Garcia Aranda** (Spain) 6

 Game 40

THE GAME: Harry Kewell scored a spectacular goal to take Leeds into the quarter-finals of a European competition for the first time in 25 years. After bravely holding out for a goalless draw in Italy seven days earlier, United's defence again held firm against one of the most dangerous strikeforces in Europe with Alf-Inge Haaland deputising magnificently for the injured Jonathan Woodgate. Roma had two men sent-off but always posed a threat through the dangerous Francesco Totti. Leeds held on though and the fans went wild at the final whistle.

LEEDS GOAL: Kewell (67 mins): Kewell shimmied away from Tommasi and his low shot found the corner of the Roma goal.

MATCH RATING: ★★★★ **LEAGUE POSITION:** 2nd

> "We don't need the Italians to tell us about Kewell's quality. Vicente Montella is a £16 million player and there is no difference in quality." DAVID O'LEARY

LEEDS UNITED	
Martyn	6
Kelly	7
Haaland	7
Booked: 64 mins (foul)	
Radebe	7
Harte	6
Bowyer	6
Bakke	7
Subbed: 84 mins (Jones)	
McPhail	7
Subbed: 89 mins (Huckerby)	
Wilcox	7
Bridges	7
Booked: 40 mins (unsporting behaviour); Subbed: 82 mins (Smith)	
Kewell ⊙	☆ 8
Goal: 67 mins	
sub: Smith	
Booked: 90 mins (foul)	
sub: Jones	
sub: Huckerby	

Subs not used: Hopkin, Mills, Duberry, Robinson.

AS ROMA	
Antonioli	6
Zago	7
Booked: 69 mins (foul); Sent-off: 90 mins (second bookable offence: foul)	
Aldair	7
Mangone	6
Rinaldi	7
Nakata	7
Subbed: 77 mins (Di Francesco)	
Tommasi	7
Candela	6
Booked: 40 mins (unsporting behaviour); Sent-off: 90 mins (violent conduct)	
Totti	☆ 8
Booked: 23 mins (foul)	
Montella	6
Delvecchio	7
Booked: 60 mins (unsporting behaviour)	
sub: Di Francesco	

Subs not used: Zanetti, Lanzaro, Lupatelli, Blasi, Tomic, Gurenko.

MATCH FACTS	
Shots On Target	
Leeds	5-4 AS Roma
Shots Off Target	
Leeds	5-14 AS Roma
Hit Woodwork	
Leeds	0-0 AS Roma
Corners	
Leeds	3-6 AS Roma

HOW THEY LINED UP

Martyn

Kelly Haaland Radebe Harte

Bowyer Bakke McPhail Wilcox

Bridges Kewell

Delvecchio Montella

Tommasi Totti Nakata

Candela Mangone Aldair Zago Cafu

Antonioli

KEWELL 10

THE FINAL SCORE!

MARCH 5		
Aston Villa	1-1	Arsenal
Leeds	3-0	Coventry
Leicester	5-2	Sunderland
MARCH 8		
West Ham	2-0	Southampton

TOP OF THE PREMIERSHIP

	P	W	D	L	Pts
1. Man. United	27	17	7	3	58
2. Leeds	27	17	3	7	54
3. Chelsea	27	14	7	6	49
4. Liverpool	26	14	6	6	48

Bradford City	(0)	**1**
Leeds United	(1)	**2**

Competition: FA Carling Premiership

Date: **Sunday March 12, 2000**

Attendance: **18,276**

Referee: **P Durkin** (Portland) 8

Game 41

THE GAME: Leeds kept the Premiership title race alive with a victory over bitter local rivals Bradford City. Michael Bridges clinched the points for David O'Leary's men with a double strike to cut the gap on Manchester United at the top of the table to four points. The battling Bantams pulled a goal back through Peter Beagrie during the second half, but it was not enough to save their six-month unbeaten league run at Valley Parade. The result leaves City struggling in the bottom three.

BRADFORD GOAL: Beagrie *(74 mins):* McCall played a short free-kick to Beagrie, who blasted a left-footed drive from 30 yards into the top right-hand corner of the net.

LEEDS GOALS: Bridges *(12 mins):* Bundled a weak six-yard shot beyond Southall after latching onto Harte's out-swinging free-kick; **Bridges** *(63 mins):* Slammed the ball into the roof of the net from close range after picking up Smith's clever pass.

MATCH RATING: ★★★ **LEAGUE POSITION: 2nd**

> "I want us to get into the Champions League. That's where the big boys are and that's where I want us to be." DAVID O'LEARY

BRADFORD CITY		LEEDS UNITED	
Southall	6	Martyn	7
McCall	7	Kelly	6
Wetherall ▢	6	Harte ▢	7
Booked: 48 mins (foul)		*Booked: 43 mins (foul)*	
Lawrence ▢	6	Haaland ▢	5
Booked: 87 mins (foul)		*Booked: 55 mins (foul)*	
Whalley	5	Radebe	8
Subbed: 66 mins (Blake)		Bridges ⊕⊕	★ 9
Beagrie ⊕	6	*Goals: 12, 63 mins; Subbed: 90 mins*	
Goal: 74 mins		*(Huckerby)*	
O'Brien	7	Bowyer	6
Windass ▢	7	McPhail	6
Booked: 79 mins (foul)		*Subbed: 72 mins (Hopkin)*	
Halle	5	Wilcox	6
Subbed: 66 mins (Cadete)		Smith	7
Jacobs ▢	7	Bakke	6
Booked: 67 mins (foul)		*sub: Hopkin*	
Saunders	★ 8	*sub: Huckerby*	
sub: Blake	5	**Subs not used:** Robinson, Duberry,	
sub: Cadete	5	Maybury.	
Subs not used: Taylor, Sharpe, Dreyer.			

MATCH FACTS			HOW THEY LINED UP
Shots On Target			
Bradford 4-5 Leeds			
Shots Off Target			
Bradford 9-8 Leeds			
Hit Woodwork			
Bradford 0-0 Leeds			
Corners			
Bradford 6-5 Leeds			

United emerged victorious at Valley Parade in the Yorkshire derby.

Leeds took a commanding hold of the quarter-final first leg tie against Slavia Prague.

Leeds United (1) 3
Slavia Prague (0) 0

Competition: **UEFA Cup Q-Final 1st Leg**

Date: **Thursday March 16, 2000**

Attendance: **39,519**

Referee: **M Merk** (Germany) 7

Game 42

THE GAME: Leeds have one foot in the semi-finals of the UEFA Cup after a professional demolition job on the below-par Czechs. Lucas Radebe and Alf-Inge Haaland were solid in the Leeds defence, denying Slavia Prague the all-important away goal to take back to the Czech Republic for the second leg. A three goal lead should be enough to steer O'Leary's young guns through to the club's first semi-final in European football since finishing as runners-up in the 1975 European Cup Final. Jason Wilcox scored the first goal and had an outstanding game on the left-wing, with Harry Kewell and Lee Bowyer adding second-half goals to give their side breathing space. All three goalscorers were in inspired form for United as they brushed aside Prague's challenge and put themselves in a commanding position for the return fixture. The visitors' misery was complete when their captain Karel Rada was sent-off for a second bookable offence 14 minutes from the end.

LEEDS GOALS: Wilcox (39 mins): Wilcox made an excellent run down the left and was picked out by Bowyer's superb pass. He sprinted into Slavia Prague's penalty box and fired in an unstoppable shot from 12 yards; **Kewell** (54 mins): From a pass by Bridges, Bakke rode two challenges to the right of goal before squaring to Kewell, who scored with ease from eight yards; **Bowyer** (59 mins): Bridges used Wilcox as a foil near the touchline and found Bowyer with a deep cross-field ball. The midfielder's well-timed run was rewarded when he finished decisively from eight yards.

MATCH RATING: ★★★ LEAGUE POSITION: 2nd

MATCH FACTS

Shots On Target
Leeds 12-5 Slavia Prague

Shots Off Target
Leeds 2-4 Slavia Prague

Hit Woodwork
Leeds 0-0 Slavia Prague

Corners
Leeds 5-2 Slavia Prague

HOW THEY LINED UP

Martyn

Kelly Haaland Radebe Harte

Bowyer Bakke McPhail Wilcox

Bridges Kewell

Kuchov Dosek, T

Petrous Doshlek Ulich

Horvath Vicek Rada Dosek, L Koller

Cerny

LEEDS UNITED

Martyn	7
Kelly	7
Haaland	8
Radebe	7
Harte	7
Bakke	6
Bowyer ⊕ ☐	7
Goal: 59 mins; Booked: 64 mins (foul)	
McPhail	6
Subbed: 78 mins (Huckerby)	
Wilcox ⊕	☆ 9
Goal: 39 mins	
Bridges	7
Subbed: 87 mins (Smith)	
Kewell ⊕	6
Goal: 54 mins	
sub: Huckerby	
sub: Smith	

Subs not used: *Hopkin, Duberry, Robinson, Mills, Jones.*

SLAVIA PRAGUE

Cerny	6
Dosek, T	6
Dosek, L	☆ 7
Vlcek	6
Subbed: 55 mins (Vagner)	
Ulich ☐	6
Booked: 82 mins (foul)	
Dostalek	6
Subbed: 65 mins (Hysky)	
Horvath	6
Petrous ☐	6
Booked: 32 mins (foul)	
Rada ☐ ▰	5
Booked: 74 mins (dissent); Sent-off: 76 mins (second bookable offence: foul)	
Koller	6
Kuchar	6
sub: Vagner	6
sub: Hysky	5

Subs not used: *Lerch, Kozel, Skala, Baclavik, Bozabel.*

THE FINAL SCORE!

MARCH 11		
Aston Villa	1-0	Coventry
Chelsea	1-1	Everton
Liverpool	1-1	Sunderland
Man. United	3-1	Derby
Newcastle	1-0	Watford
Sheff. Wed.	3-1	West Ham
Tottenham	7-2	Southampton
Wimbledon	2-1	Leicester
MARCH 12		
Bradford	1-2	**Leeds**
Middlesbrough	2-1	Arsenal
MARCH 15		
Coventry	1-0	Everton
Liverpool	0-0	Aston Villa
MARCH 18		
Coventry	4-0	Bradford
Derby	0-2	**Liverpool**
Leicester	0-2	**Man. United**
Southampton	2-0	Aston Villa
Sunderland	1-1	Middlesbrough
Watford	1-0	Sheff. Wed
West Ham	0-0	Chelsea

TOP OF THE PREMIERSHIP

	P	W	D	L	Pts
1. Man. United	29	19	7	3	64
2. Leeds	28	18	3	7	57
3. Liverpool	29	15	8	6	53
4. Chelsea	28	14	9	6	51

Harry was mortified when he slipped on a banana skin at such an important moment!

Leeds United (3) 4
Wimbledon (1) 1

Competition: FA Carling Premiership
Date: Sunday March 19, 2000
Attendance: 39,256
Referee: A Wiley (Burntwood) 7

 Game 43

THE GAME: Leeds recovered from an early Jason Euell goal to storm past the hapless Dons and gain revenge for the 2-0 defeat at Selhurst Park earlier in the season. The Wimbledon defence was continually torn apart by the pace and skill of Harry Kewell and Jason Wilcox, but it was Eirik Bakke who stood out, scoring his first goals in the Premierhip to cap off a superb performance in midfield. In sharp contrast to Leeds' sparkling form, Wimbledon look to be in real trouble on this evidence unless they can tighten up their back line.

LEEDS GOALS: Bakke (23 mins): Controlled McPhail's chip on his thigh before flicking the ball past the goalkeeper; **Harte** (28 mins, penalty): Sent Sullivan the wrong way after Cort had handled Hopkin's corner; **Bakke** (39 mins): Got a deft touch on a cross from McPhail to steer the ball home; **Kewell** (83 mins): Set off on a run from the halfway line, created room for a shot, then blasted home to make it 4-1.
WIMBLEDON GOAL: Euell (2 mins): Left-wing cross from Gayle was met with a powerful near post header.

MATCH RATING: ★★★ **LEAGUE POSITION:** 2nd

> "We are a better team than Wimbledon but we had to prove it. We're going to go out and try and win every game from now on in and see what happens."
> DAVID O'LEARY

LEEDS UNITED
Martyn	7
Kelly	6
Haaland	7
Radebe	6
Harte ⊕	6
Goal: 28 mins (pen)	
Bakke ⊕⊕	☆8
Goals: 23, 39 mins; Subbed: 85 mins (Jones)	
Hopkin	7
McPhail	7
Wilcox	7
Kewell ⊕	7
Goal: 83 mins; Subbed: 84 mins (Huckerby)	
Bridges	6
Subbed: 64 mins (Smith)	
sub: Smith	6
sub: Huckerby	
sub: Jones	

Subs not used: Robinson, Duberry.

WIMBLEDON
Sullivan	☆8
Cunningham	6
Kimble	6
Cort	6
Subbed: 46 mins (Badir)	
Earle ▯	7
Booked: 88 mins (foul)	
Euell ⊕	7
Goal: 2 mins	
Gayle	7
Ardley	6
Willmott	6
Andersen	6
Lund	6
Subbed: 65 mins (Hughes)	
sub: Badir	6
sub: Hughes	6

Subs not used: Blackwell, Heald, Anderson.

MATCH FACTS
Shots On Target
Leeds 9-5 Wimbledon
Shots Off Target
Leeds 12-8 Wimbledon
Hit Woodwork
Leeds 1-0 Wimbledon
Corners
Leeds 10-2 Wimbledon

HOW THEY LINED UP
Martyn
Kelly Haaland Radebe Harte
Hopkin McPhail Bakke Wilcox
Bridges Kewell
Cort Gayle
Ardley Earle Euell Andersen
Kimble Lund Willmott Cunningham
Sullivan

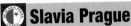

Slavia Prague	**(0) 2**
Leeds United	**(0) 1**

Leeds win 4-2 on aggregate.

Competition: UEFA Cup Q-F 2nd Leg

Date: Thursday March 23, 2000

Attendance: 13,460

Referee: O Sarvan (Turkey) 7

Game 44

THE GAME: David O'Leary's side lost the second leg of this quarter-final, but still booked their place in the semi-final of the UEFA Cup with a 4-2 aggregate win against Slavia Prague. Both sides started the match brightly, with Harry Kewell and Michael Bridges wasting good opportunities in the first half for the visitors. In the second period the game began to open up, with Slavia Prague playing some excellent attacking football. Ivo Ulich was inspirational, scoring their equaliser after Harry Kewell had put Leeds ahead just after the break. Leeds fans will be happy with the result, but in the post-match analysis David O'Leary was concerned that his team had conceded two sloppy goals, something he put down to inexperience.

SLAVIA PRAGUE GOALS: Ulich *(52 mins):* A clinical strike in the right-hand corner, sending Martyn the wrong way; **Ulich** (penalty 79 mins): Zelenka was brought down in the box by Harte. Ulich made no mistake from the spot, firing his shot into the corner with Martyn getting a touch on the ball.

LEEDS GOAL: Kewell *(47 mins):* Wilcox played a good ball to Kewell, who scored with a fantastic first-time strike from the edge of the Slavia box to put Leeds in front.

MATCH RATING: ★★★ **LEAGUE POSITION:** 2nd

SLAVIA PRAGUE			LEEDS UNITED	
Cerny	7		Martyn	7
Kozel	6		Woodgate	8
Dosek, L	7		Haaland	7
Koller	7		Radebe	8
Hysky	7		Kelly	7
Ulich ⚽⚽	⭐ 9		Bakke	7
Goals: 52, 79 mins			Jones	6
Dostalek	7		McPhail	7
Subbed: 53 mins (Vagner)			Harte	7
Skala	7		Bridges	8
Dosek, T	7		*Subbed: 49 mins (Smith)*	
Subbed: 53 mins (Lerch)			Kewell ⚽	⭐ 8
Kuchar	8		*Goal: 47 mins*	
Subbed: 85 mins (Vozabal)			*sub: Smith*	7
Zelenka	8		*Subs not used: Robinson, Hopkin,*	
sub: Vagner	6		*Huckerby, Wilcox, Mills, Duberry.*	
sub: Lerch 🟨	6			
Booked: 74 mins (foul)				
sub: Vozabal				
Subs not used: Vaclavik, Kristofik.				

MATCH FACTS

Shots On Target
Slavia Prague 6-6 Leeds

Shots Off Target
Slavia Prague 6-7 Leeds

Hit Woodwork
Slavia Prague 1-0 Leeds

Corners
Slavia Prague 3-6 Leeds

HOW THEY LINED UP

Cerny

Hysky Kozel Koller

Dosek, L Ulich Dosalek Skala Kuchar

Dosek, T Zelenka

Kewell Bridges

McPhail Bakke Haaland Jones

Harte Woodgate Radebe Kelly

Martyn

Michael Bridges' efforts weren't enough to earn a share of the points at Filbert Street.

Leicester City (1) 2
Leeds United (1) 1

Competition: FA Carling Premiership
Date: Sunday March 26, 2000
Attendance: 21,095
Referee: S Lodge (Barnsley) 7

Game 45

THE GAME: Leeds effectively threw away their chances of winning the Premiership title after a sluggish performance at Filbert Street against Leicester. The home side won the battle in midfield and Stan Collymore, who scored a well-taken goal after only 14 minutes, was a constant threat in attack for The Foxes. For The Whites, Harry Kewell showed glimpses of his sublime skill and scored an excellent individual goal to pull the score back to 1-1 before the break. However, Leeds appeared to be suffering from jet-lag after the midweek victory against Slavia Prague in the UEFA Cup and were defeated by Steve Guppy's goal early in the second half.

LEICESTER GOALS: Collymore *(14 mins):* Scored with a thunderous strike from 15 yards which left 'keeper Martyn floundering as the ball crashed into the top right-hand corner of the net; Guppy *(48 mins):* From Oakes' free-kick, Guppy found space on the left and fired the ball past Martyn.
LEEDS GOAL: Kewell *(38 mins):* Threaded his way delicately through three Leicester defenders and slotted the ball past the 'keeper at the near post from an acute angle.

MATCH RATING: ★★★★ **LEAGUE POSITION:** 2nd

"The best team are winning the league and we are doing great to be where we are. The priority remains qualifying for the Champions League." DAVID O'LEARY

MATCH FACTS
Shots On Target
Leicester 3-2 Leeds
Shots Off Target
Leicester 6-4 Leeds
Hit Woodwork
Leicester 0-1 Leeds
Corners
Leicester 2-3 Leeds

HOW THEY LINED UP

LEICESTER CITY
Flowers	7
Sinclair	7
Subbed: 46 mins (Gilchrist)	
Taggart	8
Izzet	8
Lennon	7
Booked: 58 mins (foul)	
Collymore	☆ 9
Goal: 14 mins; Booked: 90 mins (unsporting behaviour)	
Eadie	7
Subbed: 66 mins (Cottee)	
Guppy	8
Goal: 48 mins	
Savage	8
Elliott	7
Oakes	7
sub: Gilchrist	7
sub: Cottee	7

Subs not used: Impey, Marshall, Arphexad.

LEEDS UNITED
Martyn	7
Kelly	6
Harte	8
Booked: 68 mins (foul)	
Haaland	8
Booked: 90 mins (foul)	
Radebe	7
Woodgate	7
Bridges	6
Subbed: 71 mins (Huckerby)	
Kewell	☆ 8
Goal: 38 mins	
McPhail	7
Wilcox	8
Bakke	7
sub: Huckerby	

Subs not used: Maybury, Robinson, Mills, Duberry.

THIS WEEK...

IN THE NEWS
LEEDS UNITED: Eirik Bakke is rewarded for some impressive performances in the Premiership with a call up to the senior Norway squad for their Euro 2000 warm up against Switzerland. ... The press and David O'Leary believe that the defeat at Leicester has handed the championship to Man. United. The bookmakers have now placed The Red Devils at 1/14 on to retain their crown... Defender Jonathan Woodgate is back in training after recovering from a calf injury and could feature in the crucial game with Chelsea but it now seems that David Batty will be out for the rest of the season.

PREMIERSHIP: Deadline day for Premiership signings comes and goes with no real surprises or big money buys. Top spenders are Peter Reid's Sunderland, who pay £1.6 million for Milton Nunez from PAOK Salonika... The Black Cats end a disastrous run of twelve games without a victory as Kevin Phillips grabs the winner against Everton... Jamie Redknapp marks his first game back for over four months with a headed winner against Newcastle as The Reds hit a rich vein of form at the right time... Man. United, Chelsea and Arsenal have all been linked with an audacious £18 million move for PSV Eindhoven's star striker Ruud van Nistelrooy... Everton's new signing Mark Hughes is confident that he can be a success after his shock transfer from Southampton. "I haven't come here to wind down towards retirement," said the veteran striker... Hammers boss Harry Redknapp insists he will not let Paulo Wanchope leave the club to sign for Leicester City.

THE FINAL SCORE!
MARCH 26		
Arsenal	3-0	Coventry
Leicester	2-1	Leeds
West Ham	2-1	Wimbledon

TOP OF THE PREMIERSHIP
	P	W	D	L	Pts
1. Man. United	30	20	7	3	67
2. Leeds	30	19	3	8	60
3. Liverpool	30	16	8	6	56
4. Chelsea	30	14	10	6	52

APRIL

> "It is important to show the world that we will not allow the futility of violence and personal injury to cast a shadow over football in this country." Peter Ridsdale

THERE ARE TIMES WHEN FOOTBALL BECOMES INSIGNIFICANT FOR even the most dedicated supporters. April was one of those times. After the fixture-packed month of March had pushed the players to their limits – but failed to halt the push for Premiership and European glory – United's season was thrown into despair on a tragic night in Istanbul. On the evening before their semi-final with Galatasaray – the first time the club had reached that stage of any European competition for 25 years – Leeds supporters Kevin Speight and Chris Loftus lost their lives and made football matters irrelevant.

Despite this, it was decided that the game should still go ahead, though Leeds supporters were angered when there was no formal mark of respect at the game in Turkey. David O'Leary's side, clearly affected by the tragic events, lost the match 2-0 and although they earned a creditable 2-2 draw in the return leg, the fact that their European dream had finally come to an end was tempered by the sorrow that surrounded the club.

In the Premiership, The Whites were unable to get back on track after two defeats at the end of March and extended their losing streak to four games. Suddenly, the Champions League place that had looked all but certain only a few weeks previously was now in doubt. They lost at home to Chelsea and Arsenal and away to Aston Villa as players and fans alike struggled to regain their composure. The clubs at the top of the Premiership – including Leeds' recent conquerors Chelsea and Arsenal – had started to find their form and Liverpool crept above The Whites into third place. Manchester United won the title with a month still to play, but Leeds showed dogged resilience to claw their way out of their season's darkest hour. A draw with Newcastle at St James' Park stopped the losing streak, before a 3-0 win over Sheffield Wednesday boosted Leeds' hopes of qualifying for the Champions League.

THE GAMES

Apr. 1 v **Chelsea** (h)

Apr. 6 v **Galatasaray** (a)

Apr. 9 v **Aston Villa** (a)

Apr. 16 v **Arsenal** (h)

Apr. 20 v **Galatasaray** (h)

Apr. 23 v **Newcastle** (a)

Apr. 30 v **Sheff. Wed.** (a)

TRANSFERS IN

None

TRANSFERS OUT

None

MATCH facts
Matchman Of The Month

EIRIK BAKKE
Average Rating: 7.00

83

Leeds United (0) 0
Chelsea (0) 1

Game 46

Competition: FA Carling Premiership

Date: Saturday April 1, 2000

Attendance: 40,162

Referee: J Winter (Stockton) 7

THE GAME: Jon Harley's first ever goal for Chelsea virtually confirmed Manchester United as 2000 Premiership champions as The Blues dealt a crushing blow to Leeds' rapidly fading title chances. David O'Leary's young side looked a shadow of their true selves as they slumped to a third successive defeat and can no longer take for granted a place in the Champions League next season, something that looked a certainty only a few weeks ago. Defender Frank Leboeuf was booed at every opportunity by the Elland Road faithful, having been sent-off for stamping on Harry Kewell when the teams met at Stamford Bridge earlier in the season. But it was the Frenchman who had the last laugh as he confidently shackled the Australian winger, who had surprisingly little influence on the match.

CHELSEA GOAL: Harley *(62 mins):* Sutton played a good ball to the left-hand side of the Leeds area for Harley. The England Under-21 star went past Kelly – who lost his footing as he attempted to challenge the Chelsea youngster – leaving him to continue his run unchallenged and slot the ball calmly under the body of 'keeper Martyn at the foot of the near post.

MATCH RATING: ★★★ **LEAGUE POSITION: 2nd**

> "Against the big teams our record has not been good. We have to improve our record against the top sides."
> DAVID O'LEARY

LEEDS UNITED		CHELSEA	
Martyn	6	de Goey	7
Kelly	6	Ferrer	7
Woodgate	7	Leboeuf	8
Radebe	5	Thome	7
Harte	6	Wise	7
Bowyer ☐	5	Morris ☐	7
Booked: 85 mins (dissent)		*Booked: 37 mins (foul)*	
Bakke	☆ 8	Di Matteo	7
McPhail	7	Harley ⊕	☆ 9
Wilcox	7	*Goal: 62 mins; Subbed: 88 mins (Lambourde)*	
Subbed: 74 mins (Huckerby)			
Smith ☐	5	Babayaro	7
Booked: 85 mins (foul)		Weah	5
Kewell	5	Sutton ☐	6
sub: *Huckerby*		*Booked: 90 mins (foul)*	
		sub: *Lambourde*	
Subs not used: *Haaland, Robinson, Mills, Jones.*		**Subs not used:** *Hogh, Cudicini, Dalla Bona, Zola.*	

MATCH FACTS		HOW THEY LINED UP
Shots On Target		
Leeds 5-4 Chelsea		
Shots Off Target		
Leeds 12-5 Chelsea		
Hit Woodwork		
Leeds 0-0 Chelsea		
Corners		
Leeds 12-4 Chelsea		

HOW THEY LINED UP

Martyn

Kelly   Woodgate   Radebe   Harte

Bowyer   Bakke   McPhail   Wilcox

Smith   Kewell

Sutton   Weah

Harley   Wise   Morris   Di Matteo

Babayaro   Thome   Leboeuf   Ferrer

de Goey

When football suddenly seemed unimportant, Leeds had to face an intimidating night in Istanbul.

Galatasaray (2) 2
Leeds United (0) 0

Game 47

Competition: UEFA Cup S-F 1st leg

Date: **Thursday April 6, 2000**

Attendance: **40,000**

Referee: **H Krug** (Germany) 5

THE GAME: On a night when football was irrelevant after the events in Istanbul the previous evening – when two Leeds fans lost their lives – Galatasaray took a step closer to the UEFA Cup Final. Leeds found it difficult to settle, but the home team were soon into their stride, with Romanian veteran Gheorghe Hagi pulling the strings. After going 2-0 down in the first half, Leeds were a rejuvenated side after the break but were guilty of missing chances that could cost them in the second leg at Elland Road. Bridges missed an opportunity when he was clean through and Harry Kewell's header went narrowly wide. The result was disappointing, but Leeds and their travelling fans were just glad to return home after a difficult week.

GALATASARAY GOALS: Sukur (12 mins): Arif crossed for the onrushing Sukur, who headed into the bottom right corner; **Capone** (44 mins): Galatasaray took a free-kick from the right which Radebe failed to clear to safety. The ball fell to Capone, who smashed a shot past Martyn from seven yards out.

MATCH RATING: ★★ LEAGUE POSITION: 2nd

> "I saw our players faces at half-time and I could see they were just going through the motions. They were completely intimidated by what had happened."
> **LEEDS CHAIRMAN PETER RIDSDALE**

MATCH FACTS

Shots On Target
Galatasaray 8-4 Leeds

Shots Off Target
Galatasaray 9-10 Leeds

Hit Woodwork
Galatasaray 0-0 Leeds

Corners
Galatasaray 8-6 Leeds

HOW THEY LINED UP

Taffarel

Ergun   Bulent   Popescu   Capone

Okan   Suat   Belozoglu   Hagi

Sukur   Arif

Bridges

Kewell   McPhail   Bakke   Jones   Bowyer

Harte   Woodgate   Radebe   Kelly

Martyn

GALATASARAY

Taffarel	6
Bulent	6
Popescu	6
Belozoglu	6
Arif	6
Subbed: 79 mins (Sas)	
Okan	6
Subbed: 63 mins (Unsal)	
Suat	6
Sukur ⚽	7
Goal: 12 mins	
Hagi ☆	8
Subbed: 89 mins (Ahmet)	
Capone ⚽	7
Goal: 44 mins	
Ergun	6
sub: Unsal	6
sub: Sas	
sub: Ahmet	

Subs not used: Bolukbasi, Fatih, Emre, Marcio.

LEEDS UNITED

Martyn	6
Kelly	6
Harte ▯	6
Booked: 90 mins (foul)	
Radebe	6
Woodgate	6
Bridges	6
Subbed: 75 mins (Huckerby)	
Kewell ▯ ☆	7
Booked: 20 mins (dissent)	
Bowyer ▯	6
Booked: 53 mins (foul)	
McPhail	5
Bakke	6
Jones ▯	6
Booked: 27 mins (foul); Subbed: 66 mins (Wilcox)	
sub: Wilcox	6
sub: Huckerby	

Subs not used: Haaland, Robinson, Smith, Mills, Duberry.

IN THE NEWS

LEEDS UNITED: Leeds are trying to buy a 9.9 per cent stake in Oldham Athletic which would allow the club to bypass restrictions on targeting under 16-year-olds who live further than 90 minutes from their own academy… The latest transfer rumours concern Everton's **Don Hutchison**, who has failed to agree a new Everton contract… David O'Leary is also said to be lining up a £6 million offer for the young Wimbledon and England Under-21 striker **Carl Cort**.

PREMIERSHIP: The Premiership launches new plans to fine players who step out of line up to four weeks' wages… **Karlheinz Reidle** takes over as caretaker boss at Fulham but rumour has it that the club is trying to entice French legend **Jean Tigana** to take over on a long-term basis at Craven Cottages… Leicester City new boy **Stan Collymore** breaks his leg when his studs catch in the turf as he plays a pass in the game at Derby, but the striker insists he'll be back for the start of the new season… Aston Villa forward **Benito Carbone** dismisses claims he is demanding £40,000 a week to stay at Villa Park… Bolton's **Claus Jensen** admits he could be leaving the club in the summer.

THE FINAL SCORE!

APRIL 1		
Coventry	0-3	Liverpool
Everton	4-2	Watford
Leeds	0-1	Chelsea
Man. United	7-1	West Ham
Newcastle	2-0	Bradford
Southampton	1-2	Sunderland
Wimbledon	1-3	Arsenal
APRIL 2		
Derby	3-0	Leicester
APRIL 3		
Tottenham	2-3	Middlesbrough
APRIL 5		
Sheff. Wed.	0-1	Aston Villa

TOP OF THE PREMIERSHIP

	P	W	D	L	Pts
1. Man. United	31	21	7	3	70
2. Leeds	31	19	3	9	60
3. Liverpool	31	17	8	6	59
4. Chelsea	31	15	10	6	55

The players show their togetherness at Villa Park after the tragic death of two Leeds supporters in Turkey.

Aston Villa (1) 1
Leeds United (0) 0

Competition: FA Carling Premiership

Date: Sunday April 9, 2000

Attendance: 33,889

Game 48

Referee: B Knight (Orpington) 7

THE GAME: Leeds were beaten by bogey team Aston Villa for the third time this season as everyone associated with the club struggled to come terms with the tragic events in Turkey just a few days before. David O'Leary's men have now lost their last five league and cup games, but they were impressive in patches at Villa Park. The Villa defence and in-form 'keeper David James were in uncompromising mood, reducing Leeds to ineffective long-range shots. Harry Kewell created the best chance for United, finding Michael Bridges in space after a run to the byline, but the striker somehow missed an open goal from just six yards out. When Lee Bowyer also failed to find the net with a free header Leeds knew it wouldn't be their day and left Villa Park looking tired and emotionally drained.

VILLA GOAL: Joachim (40 mins): A long pass from Barry released Joachim, who shrugged off a challenge from Kelly before racing clear of the Leeds defence to beat Martyn.

MATCH RATING: ★★★ **LEAGUE POSITION: 3rd**

> "It's easy for us to say that we deserve a Champions League place but we've got to go out there and earn it."
> DAVID O'LEARY

ASTON VILLA			LEEDS UNITED	
James	⭐ 8		Martyn	6
Ehiogu	6		Kelly	6
Samuel	7		*Booked: 44 mins (foul)*	
Booked: 70 mins (foul)			Radebe	7
Barry	7		Woodgate	6
Watson	6		Harte	7
Boateng	6		Wilcox	7
Hendrie	6		McPhail	6
Subbed: 67 mins (Thompson)			Bowyer	7
Merson	7		Bakke	6
Wright	6		Bridges	6
Joachim ⊕	7		*Subbed: 60 mins (Huckerby)*	
Goal: 40 minutes			Kewell	⭐ 8
Carbone	6		*sub: Huckerby*	7
Subbed: 61 mins (Dublin)				
sub: Ghrayib	6			
sub: Dublin	6			
sub: Thompson	6			

Subs not used: Delaney, Enckelman.

Subs not used: Haaland, Robinson, Mills, Jones.

MATCH FACTS	
Shots On Target	
Aston Villa	7-8 Leeds
Shots Off Target	
Aston Villa	5-10 Leeds
Hit Woodwork	
Aston Villa	1-0 Leeds
Corners	
Aston Villa	5-5 Leeds

HOW THEY LINED UP

James

Watson   Ehiogu   Samuel   Barry   Wright

Hendrie   Boateng   Merson

Carbone   Joachim

Kewell   Bridges

Wilcox   McPhail   Bakke   Bowyer

Harte   Radebe   Woodgate   Kelly

Martyn

THIS WEEK...

IN THE NEWS

LEEDS UNITED: United's fifth consecutive defeat sees them drop out of the top two places in the table for the first time since back in September... Leeds chairman **Peter Ridsdale** remains critical of Galatasaray's opposition to the club's plans to prevent away fans from coming to Elland Road to watch the second leg of the UEFA Cup semi-final... UEFA admit that they advised Galatasaray not to wear black armbands and not to hold a minute's silence before the first leg game after the supporters' deaths in Turkey. UEFA also take what seems an eternity before finally agreeing to Leeds' wish to ban away fans, though the Turks are allowed to bring 80 specially selected 'supporters'... England coach Kevin Keegan has all but given up hope of of **David Batty** being fit for Euro 2000 after his problems in overcoming the calf injury he suffered in November.

PREMIERSHIP: John Hartson's planned big-money move to Spurs from Wimbledon breaks down after the Welshman fails a medical... Liverpool striker **Emile Heskey** is subjected to lengthy verbal racist abuse from opposition fans in an England Under-21s play-off game against Yugoslavia in Barcelona... Tottenham captain **Sol Campbell** reveals Manchester United made a £17 million bid for him earlier in the season... Brazilian defender **Roberto Carlos** says that **David Beckham** is 'slow' and 'lacking in ability' after Manchester United's 0-0 Champions League draw with Real Madrid in the Bernabeu... Leicester striker **Stan Collymore** says he could now be fit for the end of the season after dislocating his ankle and fracturing his leg in the recent game against Derby... French Footballer Of The Year **Sylvain Wiltord** has expressed an interest in joining Arsenal.

THE FINAL SCORE!

APRIL 8		
Bradford	1-2	Southampton
Leicester	1-1	Everton
Sunderland	2-1	Wimbledon
Watford	0-0	Derby

APRIL 9		
Aston Villa	1-0	Leeds
Liverpool	2-0	Tottenham

TOP OF THE PREMIERSHIP

	P	W	D	L	Pts
1. Man. United	31	21	7	3	70
2. Liverpool	32	18	8	6	62
3. Leeds	**32**	**19**	**3**	**10**	**60**
4. Arsenal	31	17	6	8	57

Leeds United (0) 0
Arsenal (1) 4

Game 49

Competition: FA Carling Premiership

Date: Sunday April 16, 2000

Attendance: 39,307

Referee: S Dunn (Bristol) 6

THE GAME: Arsenal scorched to their seventh successive victory as Leeds, who were reduced to ten men, slumped to their sixth defeat on the trot. David O'Leary's side are now in danger of missing out on a Champions League place for next season and the Elland Road boss faces a big test to get them back on track. The defining moment was the dismissal of Ian Harte before the interval for kicking Dennis Bergkamp. This allowed The Gunners to take control and add three late goals to Thierry Henry's first-half strike. Worryingly, United have only picked up three points at home and away against title rivals Man. United, Liverpool, Chelsea and Arsenal this season.

ARSENAL GOALS: Henry (21 mins): Parlour's low cross from the right was drilled in right-footed from eight yards by Henry; **Keown** (70 mins) From a corner the ball rebounded to Keown, who reacted quickly to score past Martyn; **Kanu** (82 mins): Silvinho went on a superb weaving run and presented Kanu with a simple tap-in; **Overmars** (90 mins): Vieira headed the ball forward to Overmars, who fired home to make it 4-0.

MATCH RATING: ★★★ **LEAGUE POSITION:** 4th

LEEDS UNITED		ARSENAL	
Martyn	6	Seaman	7
Kelly	6	Dixon	7
Woodgate	6	Adams	7
Haaland	5	Keown ⊕	7
Harte ▉	5	*Goal: 70 mins*	
Sent-off: 44 mins (violent conduct).		Silvinho ▢	7
Bakke	☆ 7	*Booked: 9 mins (foul)*	
Bowyer ▢	5	Parlour	7
Booked: 76 mins (foul).		Vieira ▢	7
McPhail	5	*Booked: 31 mins (foul)*	
Kewell	6	Petit ▢	7
Smith	5	*Booked: 48 mins (foul); Subbed: 82 mins (Winterburn)*	
Bridges	5	Ljungberg	☆ 8
Subbed: 46 mins Wilcox		Bergkamp ▢	6
sub: Wilcox	6	*Booked: 26 mins (foul); Subbed: 67 mins (Kanu)*	
Subs not used: Hopkin, Huckerby, Duberry, Robinson.		Henry ⊕	7
		Goal: 21 mins; Subbed: 74 mins (Overmars)	
		sub: Kanu ⊕	6
		Goal: 82 mins	
		sub: Overmars ⊕	
		Goal: 90 mins	
		Subs not used: Malz, Manninger.	

MATCH FACTS
Shots On Target
Leeds 3-10 Arsenal
Shots Off Target
Leeds 5-7 Arsenal
Hit Woodwork
Leeds 0-1 Arsenal
Corners
Leeds 5-3 Arsenal

HOW THEY LINED UP
Martyn
Kelly — Woodgate — Haaland — Harte
Bowyer — Bakke — McPhail — Kewell
Smith — Bridges
Bergkamp — Henry
Ljungberg — Petit — Vieira — Parlour
Silvinho — Adams — Keown — Dixon
Seaman

Woodgate's form suffered towards the end of the season, so the last person he wanted to face was Thierry Henry.

88

The two teams finally joined together in a minute's silence.

Leeds United (1) 2
Galatasaray (2) 2

Galatasaray win 4-2 on aggregate.

Competition: UEFA Cup S-F 2nd Leg

Date: Thursday April 20, 2000

Attendance: 38,406

Referee: L Michel (Slovakia) 6

Game 50

THE GAME: Leeds regained some of their pride by avoiding a club record seventh successive defeat, but they still tumbled out of the UEFA Cup at the semi-final stage. Already trailing by two goals from the first leg, Leeds left themselves with little hope after conceding a fifth minute penalty to Gheorghe Hagi. Eirik Bakke hit back with a goal after 16 minutes, but deadly striker Hakan Sukur scored three minutes before half-time to virtually ensure Galatasaray's place in next month's final. Both teams had a player sent-off before the break – Harry Kewell was the first to go for what looked like an innocuous challenge on Gheorghe Popescu before Belozogou Emre was dismissed for a mistimed tackle on Lee Bowyer. Bakke made it 2-2 in the second half, but it wasn't enough to send Leeds into the final and their UEFA Cup dreams were over for another season.

LEEDS GOALS: Bakke (16 mins): Wilcox's corner on the left was met by a climbing header by Bakke; **Bakke** (68 mins): Rose at the near post to head in another corner by Wilcox.
GALATASARAY GOALS: Hagi (penalty 5 mins): Woodgate brought down Suker and Hagi's left-footed penalty easily beat Martyn; **Sukur** (42 mins): A Hagi throughball found Suker, who had space to fire past a totally unprotected Martyn.

MATCH RATING: ★★★ LEAGUE POSITION: 4th

> "It's a good learning process. The kids are making some stupid mistakes. We need someone out there with more experience, such as David Batty." DAVID O'LEARY

MATCH FACTS
Shots On Target
Leeds 17-6 Galatasaray
Shots Off Target
Leeds 10-8 Galatasaray
Hit Woodwork
Leeds 0-0 Galatasaray
Corners
Leeds 11-0 Galatasaray

HOW THEY LINED UP

Martyn
Mills — Woodgate — Radebe — Harte
Bowyer — Bakke — McPhail — Wilcox
Bridges — Kewell
Sukur — Arif
Hagi — Emre — Suat — Ergun
Capone — Bulent — Popescu — Okan
Taffarel

LEEDS UNITED
Martyn	7
Mills	5
Radebe	7
Woodgate ▢	5
Booked: 5 mins (foul)	
Harte ▢	5
Booked: 23 mins (foul); Subbed: 46 mins (Huckerby)	
Bowyer	6
Bakke ⊕ ⊕	☆ 8
Goals: 16, 68 mins	
McPhail	5
Wilcox ▢	7
Booked: 63 mins (foul)	
Bridges	6
Kewell ▬	6
Sent-off: 43 mins (foul)	
sub: Huckerby	5

Subs not used: Haaland, Hopkin, Robinson, Smith, Jones, Duberry.

GALATASARAY
Taffarel ▢	☆ 9
Booked: 74 mins (unsporting behaviour)	
Capone	7
Popescu	6
Bulent	7
Hagi ⊕	8
Goal: 5 mins	
Okan	7
Subbed: 87 mins (Sas)	
Suat ▢	7
Booked: 77 mins (foul); Subbed: 81 mins (Yildiran)	
Emre ▬	6
Sent-off: 45 mins (foul)	
Ergun	7
Arif	7
Subbed: 46 mins (Unsal)	
Sukur ⊕	8
Goal: 42 mins	
sub: Unsal	6
sub: Yildiran	
sub: Sas	

Subs not used: Akyel, Marcio, Davala, Inan.

THIS WEEK...

IN THE NEWS

LEEDS UNITED: United slip out of the Champions League places after losing to Arsenal... Galatasaray arrive in Leeds protected by 11 members of the Turkish police's special operations department... The Turks announce before the game that they will be wearing black armbands during the match as a mark of respect for the Leeds fans who died... Midfield ace **Jason Wilcox** is adamant that the season will only be a success if Leeds secure a Champions League place. "It's important to get results. If we finish second then it will be a successful season," he said.
PREMIERSHIP: Man. United's attempt to defend their Champions League crown ends in a 3-2 defeat at Old Trafford against Spanish side Real Madrid. Red Devils boss Sir Alex Ferguson makes a huge £19 million bid to PSV Eindhoven for Dutch international striker **Ruud van Nistelrooy.**

THE FINAL SCORE!

APRIL 10		
Middlesbrough	3-4	**Man. United**

APRIL 12		
Chelsea	2-1	Coventry
West Ham	2-1	Newcastle
Wimbledon	0-2	**Sheff. Wed.**

APRIL 15		
Coventry	2-0	Middlesbrough
Derby	1-2	**West Ham**
Everton	4-0	Bradford
Man. United	4-0	Sunderland
Newcastle	0-2	**Leicester**
Sheff. Wed.	1-0	Chelsea
Southampton	2-0	Watford
Tottenham	2-4	**Aston Villa**

APRIL 16		
Leeds	0-4	**Arsenal**
Wimbledon	1-2	**Liverpool**

APRIL 19		
Leicester	0-1	**Tottenham**

TOP OF THE PREMIERSHIP
	P	W	D	L	Pts
1. Man. United	33	23	7	3	76
2. Liverpool	33	19	8	6	65
3. Arsenal	32	18	6	8	60
4. Leeds	33	19	3	11	60

Both sides were desperate to win but it ended 2-2.

FROM THE PAGES OF *MATCH*

After some scintillating performances earned **HARRY KEWELL** the Matchman Of The Month award for March, he told **MATCH** all about his memorable month and Champions League hopes.

How does it feel to be the top man in March? *"Yeah, I'm delighted to be recognised as the Premiership's top player, but this reflects on the team as a whole. It just goes to show how well the team has played during March, not just me."*

Were you pleased with your own form? *"I was, but I can play better. I'm still young and I've still got a great deal to learn, but fortunately I'm at a great club which encourages you to get better so I'll keep striving to do that."*

Do you feel pressure to produce week in, week out? *"No, it's a good thing to be honest. It's nice to go out there and know people expect you to do well. I'd rather have people expecting me to play well than expecting me to play badly."*

Do you like playing as a central striker? *"Yeah, it's great. You're right up at the front so you can see exactly what's happening. It means I get more opportunities to score goals and it seems to have worked well."*

Can Leeds still get a place in the Champions League? *"Obviously we haven't had a great run of results recently, but it's important we remain positive. We've done very well this season and played some great football too. We haven't given up hope by any means, and we still think we can finish in the Premiership's top three."*

What's this – a left-footed winger who can cross the ball? He must be a cert for Euro 2000.

THIS WEEK...

IN THE NEWS

LEEDS UNITED: Peter Ridsdale denies reports that the club are about to splash out £6.4 million on Lens' former Everton midfielder **Olivier Dacourt**... **Lee Bowyer** faces FA disciplinary action after the fiery midfielder picked up his 14th domestic booking of the season against Arsenal... West Ham have rubbished reports suggesting that **Rio Ferdinand** will move to Elland Road in the summer... David O'Leary is also believed to be watching Derby's England Under-21 midfielder **Seth Johnson**. A bid may be launched for the former Crewe man if The Rams fail to beat the drop.

PREMIERSHIP: Manchester United become Premiership champions once again after they defeat Southampton 3-1 at The Dell... Arsenal make it through to the UEFA Cup Final to face Galatasaray, conquerors of Leeds United in the semi-final... Chelsea could face a points deduction if the FA act upon referee Paul Durkin's match report after the recent game with Sheffield Wednesday – several players, including **Marcel Desailly**, **Didier Deschamps** and **Emerson Thome**, vented their anger at Durkin after the final whistle.

| Newcastle United | (1) 2 |
| Leeds United | (2) 2 |

Competition: FA Carling Premiership

Date: **Sunday April 23, 2000**

Attendance: **36,460**

Referee: **D Elleray** (Harrow) 5

Game 51

THE GAME: England captain Alan Shearer took his scoring tally against Leeds to 15 goals in just 13 Premiership matches after hitting the net twice at St James' Park. As at Elland Road earlier in the season, The Magpies went two goals down, but on this occasion they managed to earn a point. Leeds striker Michael Bridges ended his ten-match goal drought with the opening strike after latching on to a poor defensive clearance from Dabizas – playing in midfield for Newcastle on the day. Bridges thought he'd scored a second goal after 17 minutes before television replays showed that he didn't get a touch on Jason Wilcox's free-kick. Leeds were cruising, even though Shearer had made it 2-1 before the break – but the Magpies skipper doubled his tally three minutes into the second half to bring the scores level. Ian Harte missed a fantastic chance to wrap up the points for Leeds when he fired wide from the penalty spot after Kewell had been bundled over in the area. But after a bad run of form, the visiting fans were boosted by an entertaining match and got their first point in six games.

NEWCASTLE GOALS: Shearer *(24 mins):* Headed in at the far post after a pinpoint left-wing cross from the overlapping Domi; **Shearer** *(48 mins):* Scrambled the ball over the line after Martyn had dropped a corner from Domi on the right-wing and Hughes had knocked the ball forward.

LEEDS GOALS: Bridges *(12 mins):* Scored with a right-foot shot from 18 yards out after Dabizas had miskicked a Wilcox cross; **Wilcox** *(17 mins):* TV replays proved he scored direct from a free-kick, with Bridges distracting goalkeeper Given.

MATCH RATING: ★★★★ LEAGUE POSITION: 4th

MATCH FACTS

Shots On Target	
Newcastle 7-5 Leeds	

Shots Off Target	
Newcastle 3-7 Leeds	

Hit Woodwork	
Newcastle 1-0 Leeds	

Corners	
Newcastle 7-6 Leeds	

NEWCASTLE UNITED

Given	6
Barton	6
Hughes	7
Helder	6
Subbed: 65 mins (Marcelino)	
Howey	5
Lee	7
Dabizas	6
Gavilan	6
Subbed: 86 mins (Fumaca)	
Domi	8
Dyer	6
Subbed: 80 mins (Maric)	
Shearer ⊕ ⊕ ▯	☆ 9
Goals: 24, 48 mins; Booked: 75 mins (dissent)	
sub: Marcelino	6
sub: Maric	
sub: Fumaca	
Subs not used: Harper, McClen.	

LEEDS UNITED

Martyn	5
Mills	6
Harte ▯	7
Booked: 41 mins (foul); Subbed: 77 mins (Bowyer)	
Radebe	6
Duberry	5
Haaland ▯	7
Booked: 22 mins (foul)	
McPhail	☆ 8
Bakke ▯	7
Booked: 90 mins (foul)	
Bridges ⊕	7
Goal: 12 mins; Subbed: 80 mins (Huckerby)	
Wilcox ⊕	7
Goal: 17 mins	
Kewell ▯	7
Booked: 69 mins (unsporting behaviour)	
sub: Bowyer	
sub: Huckerby	
Subs not used: Hopkin, Robinson, Smith.	

HOW THEY LINED UP

Given

Barton — Howey — Helder — Hughes

Gavilan — Lee — Dabizas — Domi

Shearer — Dyer

Kewell — Bridges

Wilcox — McPhail — Haaland — Bakke

Harte — Duberry — Radebe — Mills

Martyn

THE FINAL SCORE!

APRIL 21		
Bradford	4-4	Derby
Everton	0-0	Liverpool

APRIL 22		
Aston Villa	2-2	Leicester
Chelsea	1-1	Middlesbrough
Sheff. Wed.	0-2	**Sunderland**
Southampton	1-3	**Man. United**
Tottenham	2-0	Wimbledon
West Ham	5-0	Coventry

APRIL 23		
Aston Villa	2-2	Leicester
Watford	2-3	**Arsenal**

TOP OF THE PREMIERSHIP

	P	W	D	L	Pts
1. Man. United	34	24	7	3	79
2. Liverpool	34	19	9	6	66
3. Arsenal	33	19	6	8	63
4. Leeds	34	19	4	11	61

The Leeds boys were celebrating even before the match against Sheffield Wednesday had started!

Sheffield Wednesday (0) 0
Leeds United (1) 3

Competition: FA Carling Premiership

Date: Sunday April 30, 2000

Attendance: 23,416

Referee: R Harris (Oxford) 7

Game 52

THE GAME: Wednesday's fate was virtually sealed as Leeds boosted their hopes of a European Champions League spot with a comfortable victory in this low-key Yorkshire derby. United got off to the perfect start when David Hopkin claimed his first goal of the season after just 40 seconds, and Bridges increased the lead early in the second half with a well taken strike. But it was Kewell's third, a superb effort from outside the area with the outside of his boot, that hinted at a return to the swagger that he and his team had shown earlier in the season. Later that evening the young Australian deservedly won the PFA Young Player Of The Year award after being nominated by his fellow pros. Wednesday rarely threatened the Leeds defence and, after this performance, look doomed for the drop, despite having three games left to play.

LEEDS GOALS: Hopkin *(1 min):* Bridges won the ball in the penalty area and squared the ball to Hopkin, who side-footed it low and wide of Pressman; **Bridges** *(53 mins):* Collected the ball from Jones just outside the penalty area and curled a sweet right-footer beyond the reach of Pressman; **Kewell** *(69 mins):* Scored a stunning goal to seal a 3-0 victory, curling an inch-perfect shot with the outside of his boot – a superb piece of skill that left Pressman with no chance.

MATCH RATING: ★★★★ **LEAGUE POSITION:** 4th

MATCH FACTS

Shots On Target		
Sheff. Wed.	5-7	Leeds
Shots Off Target		
Sheff. Wed.	7-9	Leeds
Hit Woodwork		
Sheff. Wed.	0-0	Leeds
Corners		
Sheff. Wed.	2-9	Leeds

SHEFFIELD WEDNESDAY

Pressman	6
Atherton	6
Hinchcliffe	6
Jonk	7
Walker	7
Booth	6
Alexandersson	7
Subed: 76 mins (Sonner)	
Nolan	6
de Bilde	6
Subed: 76 mins (Briscoe)	
Horne	6
Quinn	☆ 8
sub: Briscoe	
sub: Sonner	

Subs not used: Sibon, Haslam, Srnicek.

LEEDS UNITED

Martyn	7
Kelly	7
Radebe	☆ 8
Hopkin ⊕	7
Goal: 1 min	
Bridges ⊕	8
Goal: 53 mins	
Kewell ⊕	8
Goal: 69 mins	
Wilcox	7
Mills	7
Bakke ▢	7
Booked: 28 mins (foul); Subbed: 69 mins (Haaland)	
Jones	7
Duberry	8
sub: Haaland	6
sub: Huckerby	

Subs not used: Woodgate, Robinson, Smith.

HOW THEY LINED UP

Pressman

Nolan Walker Atherton Hinchcliffe

Horne Jonk Alexandersson Quinn

de Bilde Booth

Kewell Bridges

Wilcox Jones Hopkin Bakke

Kelly Duberry Radebe Mills

Martyn

IN THE NEWS

LEEDS UNITED: David O'Leary says he would love to be able to sign a striker with the profile of **Ruud van Nistelrooy**, who looks set to move to Manchester United for £19 million... UEFA announce that Leeds will not be charged over an incident during the second leg of the UEFA Cup semi-final at Elland Road when Galatasaray star striker **Hakan Sukur** was hit by a coin thrown from the crowd.

PREMIERSHIP: Manchester United chairman Martin Edwards says the club may have to sell a striker to recoup some of the money spent on **Ruud van Nistelrooy**. Days later, the transfer collapses when the Dutchman fails a medical at Old Trafford... Charlton clinch the First Division championship with a 1-1 draw at Blackburn... **Marc Overmars** has been linked with a transfer to Spanish giants Barcelona, with Ronald and Frank de Boer said to be going in the other direction... Liverpool are said to be interested in **Christian Karembeu** – but Middlesbrough are also keen to bring the French international to England.

THE FINAL SCORE!

APRIL 24		
Derby	2-0	Southampton
Man. United	3-2	Chelsea
Sunderland	0-1	**Bradford**

APRIL 29		
Aston Villa	1-1	Sunderland
Chelsea	2-0	Liverpool
Everton	0-1	**Arsenal**
Newcastle	2-0	Coventry
Southampton	1-2	**Leicester**
Tottenham	1-1	Derby
Watford	2-3	**Man. United**
West Ham	0-1	**Middlesbrough**

APRIL 30		
Bradford	3-0	Wimbledon
Sheff. Wed.	0-3	**Leeds**

TOP OF THE PREMIERSHIP

	P	W	D	L	Pts
1. Man. United	36	26	7	3	85
2. Arsenal	34	20	6	8	66
3. Liverpool	35	19	9	7	66
4. Leeds	35	20	4	11	64

MAY

"I thought that Liverpool had gained third position, then they gave it back to us! One of the highlights of the season was hearing that final whistle at West Ham." David O'Leary

AFTER CRASHING OUT OF EUROPE, AND WITH THE PREMIERSHIP
title already beyond them, the Leeds youngsters could have been forgiven
for feeling deflated after showing some superb early-season form to take
them to the top of the league. But David O'Leary needed to keep his team
focused on qualifying for a Champions League slot after they dropped into
fourth place following a disastrous month in April in which The Whites only
picked up four points out of a possible twelve.

If there was any consolation from the bitter disappointment Leeds had
suffered in the previous month, it was that they could now focus on the
Premiership. It wouldn't be easy though – O'Leary needed his experienced
players to pull the youngsters through this crucial stage of the season and
maintain their motivation and commitment. Leeds were clearly missing the
influence of David Batty, who was struggling with his ankle injury despite
months of speculation that he was about to make a return to the first team.

With only three games of the season left to go – against Watford, Everton
and West Ham – it was always going to be close, but Leeds seemed to have
an easier run-in than other teams even though they were in fourth place at
the start of May. Arsenal and Liverpool, in particular, were enjoying an
excellent run of form, and as Arsenal claimed second place it emerged that
the Merseyside giants would push The Whites all the way for third place.

Leeds got a confidence-boosting 3-1 win at Elland Road against Watford,
but a draw with Everton, in which three players were sent-off, took the fight
for third place to the final game. Leeds knew they needed a better result
against West Ham than Liverpool could earn away at Bradford. So after
drawing 0-0 with The Hammers, they faced an anxious wait before realising
they had reached their target of Champions League football for 2000-2001.

THE GAMES

May 3 v **Watford** (h)

May 8 v **Everton** (h)

May 14 v **West Ham** (a)

TRANSFERS IN

None

TRANSFERS OUT

None

MATCH facts
Matchman Of The Month

JONATHAN WOODGATE
Average Rating: 7.33

United brushed aside Watford in their quest for Champions League football next season.

Leeds United (2) 3
Watford (1) 1

Competition: FA Carling Premiership

Date: Wednesday May 3, 2000

Attendance: 36,324

Referee: P Alcock (Halstead) 7

Game 53

THE GAME: Leeds gave their prospects of qualifying for the Champions League a huge lift with a convincing victory over relegated Watford as Liverpool slipped up against Leicester. David O'Leary's team were back to something approaching the form that made them serious title contenders earlier in the campaign. Lee Bowyer was exceptional in midfield, Michael Bridges achieved his target of notching 20 goals (scored in all competitions), and there were rare strikes from Michael Duberry and Darren Huckerby – with the latter grabbing his first goal since September. Dominic Foley scored a first-half equaliser for The Hornets, but the visitors rarely threatened a determined Leeds team and were thwarted in the second half by the excellent form of United 'keeper Nigel Martyn.

LEEDS GOALS: Bridges *(20 mins):* Clever play by Bowyer allowed Bridges to fire home from just inside the penalty area for his 18th Premiership goal; **Duberry** *(45 mins):* McPhail's free-kick from the left eluded Watford's defence and Duberry blasted home from two yards; **Huckerby** *(53 mins):* Martyn's long kick was flicked on by Kewell to Huckerby, who beat defender Page and curled the ball just inside the far post.

WATFORD GOAL: Foley *(25 mins):* Helguson rose above the Leeds defence to head the ball back for Foley, who shot past Martyn from 12 yards to bring Watford level in the first half.

MATCH RATING: ★★★★ **LEAGUE POSITION: 3rd**

LEEDS UNITED			WATFORD		
Martyn		7	Day		6
Kelly		6	Cox		6
Radebe		6	Page		5
Subbed: 46 mins (Woodgate)			Ward		5
Duberry ⚽		8	Robinson		5
Goal: 45 mins			Foley		6
Mills		7	*Subbed: 66 mins (Mooney)*		
Bowyer	★	8	Hyde 🟨		7
Bakke		7	*Booked: 37 mins (foul)*		
McPhail		7	Palmer	★	8
Kewell		7	Perpetuini		7
Huckerby ⚽		8	Helguson ⚽		5
Goal: 53 mins; Subbed: 80 mins (Smith)			*Goal: 25 mins; Subbed: 66 mins (Wooter)*		
Bridges ⚽🟨		7	Smith		7
Goal: 20 mins; Booked: 37 mins (dissent)			sub: Mooney		6
sub: Woodgate		8	sub: Wooter		6
sub: Smith					

Subs not used: Robinson, Hopkin, Wilcox.

Subs not used: Chamberlain, Bonnot, Gibbs.

MATCH FACTS		
Shots On Target		
Leeds	4-5	Watford
Shots Off Target		
Leeds	10-4	Watford
Hit Woodwork		
Leeds	0-0	Watford
Corners		
Leeds	7-5	Watford

HOW THEY LINED UP

Martyn

Mills · Radebe · Duberry · Kelly

Bowyer · Bakke · McPhail · Kewell

Bridges · Huckerby

Foley · Helguson

Perpetuini · Hyde · Palmer · Smith

Robinson · Page · Ward · Cox

Day

THIS WEEK...

IN THE NEWS

LEEDS UNITED: Michael Bridges' 20th goal of the season against Watford wins him a £20 bet made pre-season with United's chief scout Ian Broomfield... Celtic's Australian striker **Mark Viduka** accepts his future may lie outside of Scotland. The revelation alerts several Premiership managers including Leeds supremo David O'Leary. Viduka scored 27 league goals this season for Celtic and was named Scotland's Player Of The Year... **Robert Molenaar**, who is recovering from cruciate knee ligament operations which have kept him out for 16 months, has signed a one-year extension to his current contract... PSV Eindhoven midfielder **Mark Van Bommel** is being watched by the club.

PREMIERSHIP: John Hartson says Wimbledon boss Egil Olsen should quit as the club's terrible run of form continues – Olsen is sacked the following day by the Wimbledon board... The future of Middlesbrough's on-loan Brazilian **Juninho** is thrown into doubt as his Spanish side Atletico Madrid are relegated. Boro chief Bryan Robson seems undecided about offering the player a permanent move... **Roy Keane** is named as the Footballer Of The Year for his outstanding performances for Manchester United this season... West Ham striker **Paolo di Canio** says he doesn't know what more he can do to make the Italy squad for Euro 2000 after a fantastic season for The Hammers.

THE FINAL SCORE!

MAY 2		
Arsenal	2-1	West Ham
Middlesbrough	2-2	Newcastle

MAY 3		
Leeds	3-1	Watford
Liverpool	0-2	Leicester

TOP OF THE PREMIERSHIP

	P	W	D	L	Pts
1. Man. United	36	26	7	3	85
2. Arsenal	35	21	6	8	69
3. Leeds	36	21	4	11	67
4. Liverpool	35	19	9	7	66

Leeds United (1) 1
Everton (0) 1

Competition: **FA Carling Premiership**

Date: **Monday May 8, 2000**

Attendance: **37,713**

Referee: **A D'Urso** (Billericay) 5

Game 54

THE GAME: Nigel Martyn may have cost his team a place in the Champions League next season after a terrible blunder on the hour that led to Everton's equaliser. Martyn's mistake let in the grateful Nick Barmby, who cancelled out Michael Bridges' first-half effort and denied Leeds three crucial points. Everton finished the game with only nine men following the dismissals of Richard Dunne and Don Hutchison, and Leeds lost Michael Duberry – sent-off for a second bookable challenge in a match which suffered from the fussy refereeing of Andy D'Urso. The draw at Elland Road means Leeds need a better result in their final game at West Ham than Liverpool achieve at Bradford to clinch third place and the vital Champions League spot.

LEEDS GOAL: Bridges (30 mins): Managed to beat Everton's offside trap before shooting past Gerrard from six yards out.

EVERTON GOAL: Barmby (60 mins): Hutchison lofted a ball into the Leeds penalty area, where 'keeper Martyn misjudged the bounce. The ball ran to Barmby, who shot home from the narrowest of angles.

MATCH RATING: ★★★ LEAGUE POSITION: 3rd

LEEDS UNITED		
Martyn		5
Kelly		7
Duberry ☐ ■		6
Booked: 18 mins (foul); Sent-off: 54 mins (second bookable offence: foul)		
Woodgate		7
Mills		6
Bowyer		6
Bakke		☆ 8
McPhail		6
Wilcox		7
Subbed: 56 mins (Haaland)		
Bridges ⊕		7
Goal: 30 mins; Subbed: 81 mins (Huckerby)		
Kewell		7
sub: Haaland		6
sub: Huckerby		
Subs not used: Hopkin, Jones, Robinson.		

EVERTON		
Gerrard		6
Dunne ■		6
Sent-off: 50 mins (violent conduct)		
Unsworth ☐		7
Booked: 65 mins (foul)		
Weir		6
Ball ☐		6
Booked: 17 mins (foul)		
Pembridge		7
Subbed: 79 mins (Ward)		
Hughes, S ☐		6
Booked: 87 mins (foul)		
Collins		7
Barmby ⊕ ☐		7
Goal: 60 mins; Booked: 74 mins (foul)		
Hutchison ☐ ■		☆ 8
Booked: 45 mins (foul); Sent-off: 87 mins (second bookable offence: dissent)		
Hughes, M ☐		7
Booked: 35 mins (foul); Subbed 73 mins (Cadamarteri)		
sub: Cadamarteri		
sub: Ward		
Subs not used: Jevons, Clarke, Simonsen.		

MATCH FACTS
Shots On Target
Leeds 3-2 Everton
Shots Off Target
Leeds 11-6 Everton
Hit Woodwork
Leeds 0-0 Everton
Corners
Leeds 8-1 Everton

HOW THEY LINED UP

Martyn

Mills Duberry Woodgate Kelly

Bowyer Bakke McPhail Wilcox

Bridges Kewell

Hughes, M Hutchison

Barmby Collins Hughes, S Pembridge

Ball Weir Unsworth Dunne

Gerrard

Everton proved tough opponents at Elland Road to leave United sweating about their final game.

Despite Foe's late challenge on Matthew Jones, Leeds ended the season on a high.

West Ham United (0) 0
Leeds United (0) 0

Competition: FA Carling Premiership

Date: Sunday May 14, 2000

Attendance: 26,044

Referee: G Barber (Tring) 7

Game 55

THE GAME: It's been an action-packed season of highs and lows for Leeds United, but they finally made the Champions League thanks to this goalless draw at Upton Park. Chances were few and far between in a scrappy encounter as West Ham refused to let the Yorkshiremen have it all their own way. In truth, The Hammers were the better side over 90 minutes – they created better chances and deserved to win the match. Marc-Vivien Foe, playing in his last game for West Ham, was sent-off for kicking the grounded Matthew Jones. But United escaped a similar body blow by gaining a vital draw and have rivals Bradford City to thank after their crucial victory against Liverpool. While the 1-0 win preserved their own Premiership status, it also meant that Leeds – finishing above Liverpool in third place – qualified for the Champions League next season, capping a superb 1999-2000 campaign for the United faithful.

MATCH RATING: ★★★ **LEAGUE POSITION: 3rd**

> "This was a reward for a young team and I didn't think we'd make it this season. Three-quarters of the way across the ocean the engines failed and we only just limped into port." DAVID O'LEARY

MATCH FACTS
Shots On Target
West Ham 3-4 Leeds
Shots Off Target
West Ham 7-11 Leeds
Hit Woodwork
West Ham 0-0 Leeds
Corners
West Ham 3-4 Leeds

HOW THEY LINED UP

Bywater

Potts Margas Stimac Ferdinand

Moncur Foe Sinclair

Kanoute Wanchope di Canio

Kewell Bridges

Wilcox McPhail Bakke Jones

Kelly Radebe Woodgate Mills

Martyn

WEST HAM UNITED
Bywater	7
Stimac	7
Potts	7
Margas	7
Ferdinand	☆ 8
Sinclair	6
Foe 🟥	5

Sent-off: 90 mins (violent conduct)

Moncur 🟨	7

Booked: 17 mins (foul)

di Canio	7
Kanoute 🟨	7

Booked: 64 mins (unsporting behaviour)

Wanchope	6

Subs not used: Feuer, Newton, McCann, Alexander, Forbes.

LEEDS UNITED
Martyn	7
Kelly	7
Radebe	7
Woodgate	7
Mills 🟨	7

Booked: 32 mins (dissent)

Jones	6
McPhail	☆ 8
Wilcox	6

Subbed: 88 mins (Huckerby)

Bakke	6

Subbed: 79 mins (Bowyer)

Bridges	6

Subbed: 28 mins (Smith)

Kewell	7
sub: Smith	7
sub: Bowyer 🟨	

Booked: 81 mins (foul)

sub: Huckerby	

Subs not used: Robinson, Duberry.

IN THE NEWS

LEEDS UNITED: The goalless draw with West Ham and Liverpool's loss at Bradford means **David O'Leary** fulfils his main aim for the season – a Champions League place for the new campaign... The Leeds manager is said to be interested in Scotland Under-21 international **Kenny Miller** from Hibernian... Serie A big-spenders Juventus, Inter Milan and Roma are said to be preparing bids for defender **Jonathan Woodgate**.

PREMIERSHIP: The relegation struggle proved to be even more exciting than the title race in the end, with Sheffield Wednesday, Watford and Wimbledon saying goodbye to top-flight football...

THE FINAL SCORE!

MAY 6		
Arsenal	2-1	Chelsea
Coventry	4-1	Sheff. Wed.
Derby	0-0	Newcastle
Leicester	3-0	Bradford
Man. United	3-1	Tottenham
Middlesbrough	1-1	Watford
Sunderland	1-0	West Ham
Wimbledon	2-2	Aston Villa

MAY 7		
Liverpool	0-0	Southampton

MAY 8		
Leeds	1-1	Everton

MAY 9		
Arsenal	3-3	Sheff. Wed.

MAY 14		
Aston Villa	0-1	**Man. United**
Bradford	1-0	Liverpool
Chelsea	4-0	Derby
Everton	0-2	**Middlesbrough**
Newcastle	4-2	Arsenal
Sheff. Wed.	4-0	Leicester
Southampton	2-0	Wimbledon
Tottenham	3-1	Sunderland
Watford	1-0	Coventry
West Ham	0-0	Leeds

TOP OF THE PREMIERSHIP
	P	W	D	L	Pts
1. Man. United	38	28	7	3	91
2. Arsenal	38	22	7	9	73
3. Leeds	38	21	6	11	69
4. Liverpool	38	18	11	9	65

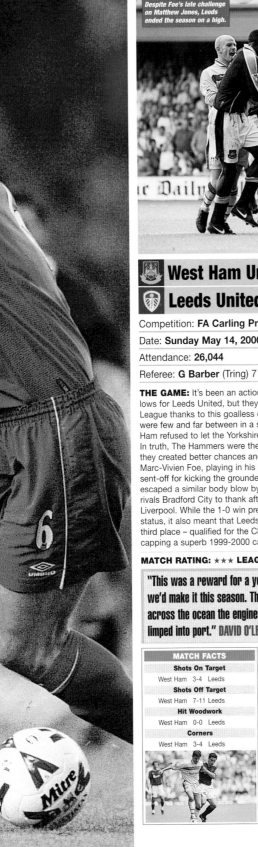

1999-2000 SQUAD Games/Goals

NAME	LGE	UC	FA	WC	TOTAL
1. Nigel **Martyn**	38/0	12/0	3/0	2/0	**55/0**
2. Gary **Kelly**	31/0	11/0	3/0	2/0	**47/0**
3. Ian **Harte**	33/6	12/1	3/1	1/0	**49/8**
4. Alf-Inge **Haaland**	13/0	6/0	0/0	0/0	**19/0**
5. Lucas **Radebe**	31/0	11/2	2/0	2/0	**46/2**
6. Jonathan **Woodgate**	34/1	10/0	3/0	2/0	**49/1**
7. David **Hopkin**	14/1	3/0	0/0	1/0	**18/1**
8. Michael **Bridges**	34/19	12/2	2/0	2/0	**50/21**
10. Harry **Kewell**	36/10	12/5	3/2	2/0	**53/17**
11. Lee **Bowyer**	33/5	11/5	3/1	1/0	**48/11**
12. Darren **Huckerby**	33/2	9/1	3/0	1/0	**46/3**
13. Paul **Robinson**	0/0	0/0	0/0	0/0	**0/0**
14. Stephen **McPhail**	23/2	9/0	3/0	2/0	**37/2**
16. Jason **Wilcox**	20/3	3/1	2/0	0/0	**25/4**
17. Alan **Smith**	26/4	8/1	3/1	1/0	**38/6**
18. Danny **Mills**	17/1	2/0	1/0	1/1	**21/2**
19. Eirik **Bakke**	29/2	10/2	3/4	2/0	**44/8**
20. Matthew **Jones**	11/0	5/0	1/0	1/0	**18/0**
21. Martin **Hiden**	1/0	0/0	0/0	0/0	**1/0**
22. Michael **Duberry**	13/1	1/0	1/0	1/0	**16/1**
23. David **Batty**	16/0	4/0	0/0	2/0	**22/0**
24. Danny **Hay**	0/0	0/0	0/0	0/0	**0/0**
25. David **Robertson**	0/0	0/0	0/0	0/0	**0/0**
27. Alan **Maybury**	0/0	0/0	0/0	0/0	**0/0**
30. Robert **Molenaar**	0/0	0/0	0/0	0/0	**0/0**
31. Tommy **Knarvik**	0/0	0/0	0/0	0/0	**0/0**
35. Lee **Matthews**	0/0	0/0	0/0	0/0	**0/0**

Harry Kewell receiving his well-deserved Young Player Of The Year award.

PREMIERSHIP MATCHMAN OF THE SEASON

PAOLO DI CANIO WAS NAMED THE PREMIERSHIP MATCHMAN OF the season after a sensational 1999-2000 with West Ham, but he certainly didn't run away with it. In fourth place, Harry Kewell was Leeds United's Matchman Of The Season with an average rating of 7.16 out of ten. Harry won an incredible 13 star ratings and scored ten goals in the Premiership. He was also named the 2000 Football Writers' and PFA Young Footballer Of The Year. Leeds skipper Lucas Radebe had another dominant season in defence and finished in a respectable 34th place with a rating of 6.87. Eirik Bakke was just an unknown youngster from Norway until he started making the headlines with some awesome performances in the midfield. Eirik finished in joint 66th position with an average rating of 6.74. Close behind him was Jonathan Woodgate, who came of age last season with some assured performances that earnt him international recognition. Woody ended the season in 68th with a rating of 6.73, ahead of many of the Premiership's highly-rated defenders. In 98th position, Nigel Martyn was a consistent performer in goal for Leeds last season, which earned him an average rating of 6.60. Ahead of many of his more established team-mates, the promising Stephen McPhail finished in 105th place with a rating of 6.58. Attacking full-back Ian Harte was close behind with an average of 6.57 and Lee Bowyer was the final Leeds player to make the top 150 players in the Premiership with a 1999-2000 rating of 6.54.

1. **PAOLO DI CANIO** *West Ham United*	29	13	7.48
2. **Roy Keane** *Manchester United*	29	6	7.24
3. **Paul Merson** *Aston Villa*	29	10	7.17
4. **HARRY KEWELL** *Leeds United*	36	13	7.16
5. **Thierry Henry** *Arsenal*	30	8	7.16
6. **Neil Sullivan** *Wimbledon*	37	9	7.13
7. **Dean Richards** *Southampton*	35	11	7.05
8. **Tim Sherwood** *Tottenham Hotspur*	25	4	7.04
9. **Don Hutchison** *Everton*	29	6	7.03
10. **Ryan Giggs** *Manchester United*	30	5	7.03
11. **Paul Ince** *Middlesbrough*	32	10	7.00
12. **John Collins** *Everton*	34	8	7.00
13. **Chris Makin** *Sunderland*	34	5	7.00
14. **David Beckham** *Manchester United*	31	5	7.00
15. **Jaap Stam** *Manchester United*	33	2	7.00
16. **Richard Gough** *Everton*	29	2	7.00
17. **David Ginola** *Tottenham Hotspur*	36	7	6.97
18. **Carl Cort** *Wimbledon*	34	4	6.97
19. **Nikos Dabizas** *Newcastle United*	29	4	6.96
= **Sol Campbell** *Tottenham Hotspur*	29	4	6.96
21. **Patrick Vieira** *Arsenal*	30	3	6.96
22. **Darren Anderton** *Tottenham Hotspur*	22	6	6.95
23. **Jamie Redknapp** *Liverpool*	19	4	6.94
24. **Sami Hyypia** *Liverpool*	38	5	6.92
25. **Matt Elliott** *Leicester City*	37	7	6.91
26. **Muzzy Izzet** *Leicester City*	32	4	6.90
27. **Rob Lee** *Newcastle United*	30	4	6.90
28. **Ben Thatcher** *Wimbledon*	20	3	6.90
29. **Gary McAllister** *Coventry City*	38	8	6.89
30. **Niall Quinn** *Sunderland*	35	7	6.88
31. **Stefan Schwarz** *Sunderland*	27	3	6.88
32. **Martin Keown** *Arsenal*	27	0	6.88
33. **Rio Ferdinand** *West Ham United*	33	3	6.87
34. **LUCAS RADEBE** *Leeds United*	31	3	6.87
35. **Thomas Sorensen** *Sunderland*	37	4	6.86
36. **Kenny Cunningham** *Wimbledon*	37	2	6.86
37. **Kevin Phillips** *Sunderland*	36	7	6.83

38. **Neil Lennon** *Leicester City*	31	5	6.83
39. **Trevor Sinclair** *West Ham United*	36	3	6.83
40. **Fredrik Ljungberg** *Arsenal*	24	3	6.83
41. **Hermann Hreidarsson** *Wimbledon*	24	2	6.83
42. **Christian Ziege** *Middlesbrough*	29	5	6.82
43. **Mart Poom** *Derby County*	28	4	6.82
44. **Lee Dixon** *Arsenal*	28	1	6.82
45. **Magnus Hedman** *Coventry City*	35	6	6.80
46. **Juninho** *Middlesbrough*	25	6	6.80
47. **Emmanuel Petit** *Arsenal*	26	3	6.80
48. **Paul Butler** *Sunderland*	31	3	6.80
49. **Tony Adams** *Arsenal*	21	0	6.80
50. **Robbie Earle** *Wimbledon*	24	3	6.79
51. **Mark Schwarzer** *Middlesbrough*	37	7	6.78
52. **David Wetherall** *Bradford City*	38	4	6.78
53. **Chris Perry** *Tottenham Hotspur*	37	2	6.78
54. **Warren Barton** *Newcastle United*	33	2	6.78
55. **Gareth Southgate** *Aston Villa*	31	8	6.77
56. **Gustavo Poyet** *Chelsea*	31	6	6.77
57. **Marcus Gayle** *Wimbledon*	36	5	6.77
58. **Paul Scholes** *Manchester United*	31	4	6.77
59. **Gilles Grimandi** *Arsenal*	27	0	6.77
60. **Stephen Carr** *Tottenham Hotspur*	34	5	6.76
61. **Kevin Campbell** *Everton*	26	1	6.76
62. **Frank Lampard** *West Ham United*	34	0	6.76
63. **Dan Petrescu** *Chelsea*	28	4	6.75
64. **Chris Armstrong** *Tottenham Hotspur*	29	2	6.75
65. **David Seaman** *Arsenal*	24	1	6.75
66. **EIRIK BAKKE** *Leeds United*	27	4	6.74
= **Titi Camara** *Liverpool*	27	4	6.74
68. **JONATHAN WOODGATE** *Leeds United*	34	1	6.73
69. **Steve Bould** *Sunderland*	19	1	6.73
70. **Gary Speed** *Newcastle United*	36	2	6.72
71. **Oyvind Leonhardsen** *Tottenham Hotspur*	22	0	6.72
72. **Emile Heskey** *Liverpool*	35	6	6.71
73. **Matt Clarke** *Bradford City*	21	3	6.71
74. **Marc Overmars** *Arsenal*	30	7	6.70
75. **Dennis Wise** *Chelsea*	30	4	6.70
76. **Nordin Wooter** *Watford*	20	3	6.70
77. **Mustapha Hadji** *Coventry City*	33	7	6.69
78. **Alan Shearer** *Newcastle United*	36	4	6.69
79. **Andy Cole** *Manchester United*	26	4	6.69
80. **Denis Irwin** *Manchester United*	25	1	6.68
81. **Paulo Wanchope** *West Ham United*	34	6	6.67
82. **Nolberto Solano** *Newcastle United*	30	5	6.66
83. **John Moncur** *West Ham United*	21	1	6.66
84. **Brian Deane** *Middlesbrough*	29	3	6.65
= **Kieron Dyer** *Newcastle United*	29	3	6.65
86. **Pavel Srnicek** *Sheffield Wednesday*	20	3	6.65
87. **Silvinho** *Arsenal*	29	0	6.65
88. **Steven Gerrard** *Liverpool*	28	4	6.64
89. **Paul Jones** *Southampton*	31	3	6.64
90. **Ian Walker** *Tottenham Hotspur*	38	2	6.63
91. **Nigel Winterburn** *Arsenal*	22	0	6.63
92. **Nick Barmby** *Everton*	37	7	6.62
93. **Igor Stimac** *West Ham United*	24	1	6.62
94. **Seth Johnson** *Derby County*	36	5	6.61
95. **Dean Saunders** *Bradford City*	31	5	6.61
96. **Ugo Ehiogu** *Aston Villa*	31	2	6.61
= **Gianfranco Zola** *Chelsea*	31	2	6.61
98. **NIGEL MARTYN** *Leeds United*	38	2	6.60
99. **David Unsworth** *Everton*	33	2	6.60
100. **Marcel Desailly** *Chelsea*	23	2	6.60
101. **Teddy Sheringham** *Manchester United*	20	2	6.60
102. **Henning Berg** *Manchester United*	20	1	6.60
103. **Dwight Yorke** *Manchester United*	31	4	6.58
104. **Steffen Iversen** *Tottenham Hotspur*	36	3	6.58
105. **STEPHEN MCPHAIL** *Leeds United*	24	3	6.58
106. **Gerry Taggart** *Leicester City*	31	2	6.58
107. **Richard Shaw** *Coventry City*	29	2	6.58
108. **Andrew Impey** *Leicester City*	28	2	6.57
109. **Kevin Pressman** *Sheffield Wednesday*	19	2	6.57
110. **IAN HARTE** *Leeds United*	33	0	6.57
111. **Steve Guppy** *Leicester City*	30	2	6.56
112. **Didier Domi** *Newcastle United*	23	2	6.56
113. **Marc-Vivien Foe** *West Ham United*	25	1	6.56
114. **Robert Page** *Watford*	36	6	6.55
115. **Patrik Berger** *Liverpool*	34	6	6.55
116. **Mark Hughes** *Everton*	29	3	6.55
117. **Ole Gunnar Solskjaer** *Manchester United*	20	2	6.55
118. **Steve Palmer** *Watford*	38	1	6.55
119. **LEE BOWYER** *Leeds United*	31	4	6.54
120. **Michael Owen** *Liverpool*	24	3	6.54
121. **Eric Roy** *Sunderland*	22	2	6.54
= **Shaka Hislop** *West Ham United*	22	2	6.54
123. **Michael Gray** *Sunderland*	33	0	6.54
124. **Ray Parlour** *Arsenal*	30	2	6.53
125. **Paul Williams** *Coventry City*	28	2	6.53
126. **Stuart McCall** *Bradford City*	34	2	6.52
127. **Stephen Clemence** *Tottenham Hotspur*	19	1	6.52
128. **David Weir** *Everton*	34	0	6.52
129. **Jo Tessem** *Southampton*	23	0	6.52
130. **Robbie Keane** *Coventry City*	31	4	6.51
131. **Robbie Savage** *Leicester City*	35	3	6.51
132. **Jason Euell** *Wimbledon*	37	0	6.51
= **Ed de Goey** *Chelsea*	37	0	6.51
134. **Darryl Powell** *Derby County*	31	0	6.51
135. **Jacob Laursen** *Derby County*	36	2	6.50
136. **Matthew Oakley** *Southampton*	28	1	6.50
137. **Dominic Matteo** *Liverpool*	32	0	6.50
138. **Aaron Hughes** *Newcastle United*	24	0	6.50
139. **Gary Neville** *Manchester United*	22	0	6.50
140. **Robbie Blake** *Bradford City*	25	4	6.48
141. **Dietmar Hamann** *Liverpool*	27	1	6.48
142. **Nicky Butt** *Manchester United*	27	1	6.48
143. **Steve Lomas** *West Ham United*	25	1	6.48
144. **Horacio Carbonari** *Derby County*	29	0	6.48
= **Mauricio Taricco** *Tottenham Hotspur*	29	0	6.48
146. **Emerson Thome** *Chelsea*	36	5	6.47
147. **Sander Westerveld** *Liverpool*	36	3	6.47
148. **Alan Thompson** *Aston Villa*	19	2	6.47
149. **Richard Johnson** *Watford*	21	1	6.47
150. **Peter Beagrie** *Bradford City*	34	0	6.47

EIRIK BAKKE

- **Position:** Midfielder
- **Born:** September 13, 1977 in Sogndal (Norway)
- **Leeds Debut:** September 30, 1999 v Partizan Belgrade
- **Total Leeds League Apps/Goals:** 29/2
- **Transfer:** £1.75 million, May 25, 1999
- **Previous Clubs:** Sogndal
- **Club Honours:** None
- **International Honours:** Senior, Under-21 Norway international

Eirik Bakke was expected to sit on the subs bench for a while before making his debut for Leeds, but he was given a chance to shine because of David Batty's misfortune with injuries last season. Eirik wasted no time in impressing both his manager and the United faithful. Indeed, by the end of the season he had unexpectedly become one of the team's star performers. The towering Norwegian is combative in the same mould as David Batty, but he likes to get forward more than the England international, suggesting the two could be accommodated in the same midfield to good effect when Batty returns from injury. Eirik can find the back of the net as well – he was Leeds' top scorer in the FA Cup last season with four goals. He also adds some height to the side from set-pieces, joining defenders Lucas Radebe and Jonathan Woodgate as targets from corners and free-kicks. The signing of Olivier Dacourt to add to Eirik, Lee Bowyer, Stephen McPhail and Matthew Jones means there will be plenty of competition in the centre of midfield for the new campaign – a sign that David O'Leary is building an exciting squad full of quality players.

Lge Games	Total mins	Goals	Star Ratings	Ave Rating
29	2231	2	4	6.74

Starts	Subbed off	Subbed on	Yellow	Red
24	5	5	7	0

Cup	Games/Goals	Sub on/off	Star Ratings	Yellow/Red
UEFA	10/2	1/1	2	0/0
FA	3/4	0/1	1	0/0
Worthington	2/0	0/0	0	0/0

LEE BOWYER

- **Position:** Midfielder
- **Born:** January 3, 1977 in London
- **Leeds Debut:** August 17, 1996 v Derby
- **Total Leeds League Apps/Goals:** 125/21
- **Transfer:** £2.6 million, July 5, 1996
- **Previous Clubs:** Charlton Athletic
- **Club Honours:** None
- **International Honours:** England Under-21 international

A fantastic start to last season forced Lee Bowyer onto the fringe of the full England squad. His midfield displays earnt the former Charlton man rave reviews from the local and national press alike. It seemed only a matter of time before Kevin Keegan gave him the chance to impress at senior level, particularly after excelling for the Under-21s. Unfortunately, Lee had problems off the field at the beginning of 2000 and these setbacks, plus a recurrent groin injury, threatened to ruin a season that had started so well. Leeds supporters will be hoping to see the midfielder get back to his best this season because the talent is undoubtedly there. At his best, Lee is a sought-after box-to-box player that any manager would love to have in his team. He dominated some crucial matches during 1999-2000 and scored some vital goals, combining his obvious technical ability with his tireless running and fighting spirit. In giving 100 per cent for the United cause, he is often regarded as an over-aggressive player by neutral observers, but the supporters who watch him every week know this is simply his determination to succeed at the highest level.

Lge Games	Total mins	Goals	Star Ratings	Ave Rating
33	2767	5	4	6.54

Starts	Subbed off	Subbed on	Yellow	Red
31	4	2	13	0

Cup	Games/Goals	Sub on/off	Star Ratings	Yellow/Red
UEFA	11/5	0/1	2	4/0
FA	3/1	0/1	1	1/0
Worthington	1/0	0/0	0	1/0

DAVID BATTY

- **Position:** Midfielder
- **Born:** December 2, 1968 in Leeds
- **Leeds Debut:** November 21, 1987 v Swindon
- **Total Leeds League Apps/Goals:** 237/4
- **Transfer:** £4.4 million, December 2, 1998
- **Previous Clubs:** Blackburn Rovers, Newcastle United
- **Club Honours:** 1992 Division One winner with Leeds

> David played five times for Blackburn in the 1994-95 Premiership winning campaign, but he declined a winners' medal saying that he didn't feel he'd contributed enough to the cause that season.

- **International Honours:** Senior England international

After making his Leeds debut as a fresh-faced 18-year-old, David Batty soon became a crucial part of the side that returned to the top-flight before winning the last Division One championship (before the new Premier League) in 1992. His departure to Blackburn Rovers in 1993 angered the loyal fans at Elland Road who loved his never-say-die style of play. After five years away from home, Batts was delighted to return to Leeds in 1998 and he was playing some of the best football of his career until an ankle injury – sustained against Bradford City in November 1999 – put him out of action for the entire season, causing him to miss England's Euro 2000 campaign. After being diagnosed with a heart problem last season and having suffered further ankle problems, David is expected to miss the 2000-2001 season. But whatever happens now in his career, his place in the Leeds Hall Of Fame is assured.

Lge Games	Total mins	Goals	Star Ratings	Ave Rating
16	1380	0	1	6.68

Starts	Subbed off	Subbed on	Yellow	Red
16	1	0	0	0

Cup	Games/Goals	Sub on/off	Star Ratings	Yellow/Red
UEFA	4/0	0/0	1	0/0
FA	0/0	0/0	0	0/0
Worthington	2/0	0/1	1	0/0

MICHAEL **BRIDGES**

- **Position:** Striker
- **Born:** May 10, 1978 in North Shields
- **Leeds Debut:** October 8, 1999 v Derby
- **Total Leeds League Apps/Goals:** 34/19
- **Transfer:** £5 million, July 24, 1999
- **Previous Clubs:** Sunderland
- **Club Honours:** Division One winner with Sunderland
- **International Honours:** England Under-21 international

David O'Leary pipped his old mentor George Graham to bring Michael Bridges to Elland Road before the start of last season. Eyebrows were raised at the price – he became Leeds' record signing at £5 million, but Michael matches the manager's brief perfectly – he is young, gifted and British. The frontman never really got an extended run in the first team at Sunderland, but he hasn't disappointed since moving to Leeds. After grabbing a hat-trick in his second game against Southampton, Michael ended 1999-2000 as the club's top scorer with 19 goals and will be looking for an even bigger return in his second season.

Lge Games	Total mins	Goals	Star Ratings	Ave Rating
34	2341	19	3	6.34
Starts	**Subbed off**	**Subbed on**	**Yellow**	**Red**
32	19	2	6	0

Cup	Games/Goals	Sub on/off	Star Ratings	Yellow/Red
UEFA	12/2	0/10	1	2/0
FA	2/0	1/1	0	0/0
Worthington	2/0	0/2	0	1/0

MICHAEL **DUBERRY**

- **Position:** Defender
- **Born:** October 14, 1975 in Enfield
- **Leeds Debut:** August 28, 1999 v Tottenham
- **Total Leeds League Apps/Goals:** 13/1
- **Transfer:** £4.5 million, July 12, 1999
- **Previous Clubs:** Chelsea, Bournemouth (on loan)
- **Club Honours:** 1997 FA Cup winner with Chelsea
- **International Honours:** England Under-21 international

Michael Duberry joined Leeds in the close season of 1998-99 because his prospects of regular first-team football at Chelsea had become limited by Frank Leboeuf, Marcel Desailly and Jes Høgh. David O'Leary knew that he needed more cover for Lucas Radebe and Jonathan Woodgate, and although some people thought the £4.5 million fee was too expensive, Leeds fans soon realised he was an able deputy. Doobs was unlucky last season as Radebe and Woodgate maintained their form and steered clear of serious injury. These factors limited his appearances, and a thigh injury sustained in September didn't allow him to impress the manager with a prolonged run in the side. But the defender has pace, aggression and strength on the ball, and with a demanding schedule this season, the big man should have a bigger role in United's quest for silverware.

Lge Games	Total mins	Goals	Star Ratings	Ave Rating
13	1099	1	0	6.69
Starts	**Subbed off**	**Subbed on**	**Yellow**	**Red**
12	1	1	5	1

Cup	Games/Goals	Sub on/off	Star Ratings	Yellow/Red
UEFA	1/0	0/0	0	0/0
FA	1/0	0/1	0	0/0
Worthington	1/0	1/0	0	0/0

ALF-INGE **HAALAND**

- **Position:** Defender/Midfielder
- **Born:** November 23, 1972 in Stavanger (Norway)
- **Leeds Debut:** August 9, 1997 v Arsenal
- **Total Leeds League Apps/Goals:** 74/8
- **Transfer:** £1.6 million, July 17, 1997
- **Previous Clubs:** Byrne, Nottingham Forest
- **Club Honours:** None
- **International Honours:** Senior Norway international

Despite only making seven league starts last season for Leeds in a number of different positions, Alf-Inge Haaland never let anyone down when called upon. David O'Leary has decided to give the youngsters a chance to impress at Elland Road, and with a wealth of talented young midfielders in the squad, Alfie has missed out on regular first-team football. He showed his versatility in United's European games though, stepping into the back line as a central defender and even getting the nod ahead of Michael Duberry. However, at the end of the season Alfie realised that his future at Elland Road would be spent mostly on the sidelines and he remains a determined performer who needs to play at the top. His summer transfer to Manchester City should provide him with regular first-team football and the newly promoted club will benefit from signing an experienced, versatile and wholehearted professional.

Lge Games	Total mins	Goals	Star Ratings	Ave Rating
13	756	0	1	6.40
Starts	**Subbed off**	**Subbed on**	**Yellow**	**Red**
7	0	6	4	0

Cup	Games/Goals	Sub on/off	Star Ratings	Yellow/Red
UEFA	6/0	1/0	0	1/0
FA	0/0	0/0	0	0/0
Worthington	0/0	0/0	0	0/0

IAN **HARTE**

- **Position:** Defender
- **Born:** August 31, 1977 in Drogheda
- **Leeds Debut:** January 22, 1996 v West Ham
- **Total Leeds League Apps/Goals:** 98/12
- **Transfer:** From Trainee, December 15, 1995
- **Previous Clubs:** None
- **Club Honours:** None
- **International Honours:** Senior, Under-21 Republic Of Ireland international

Unlike his uncle Gary Kelly, Ian Harte didn't burst into the first team to rave reviews. But after an uncertain start the Irishman has improved immensely and has seen off challenges to his position to become one of United's most consistent players. Ian has a sound positional sense and he loves to get forward from the left-wing whenever he gets the opportunity. He also scores an impressive amount of goals for a defender, which makes him a valuable member of the side. He has become the club's penalty taker – because he is such a good striker of the ball – and scored four times from the spot last season. Hartey takes lethal, inswinging corners and a mean free-kick from anywhere around the 18-yard box. Goalkeepers will be quaking in their boots after seeing him score an impressive hat-trick of free-kicks in one memorable pre-season game.

Lge Games	Total mins	Goals	Star Ratings	Ave Rating
33	2911	6	0	6.57
Starts	**Subbed off**	**Subbed on**	**Yellow**	**Red**
33	3	0	8	1

Cup	Games/Goals	Sub on/off	Star Ratings	Yellow/Red
UEFA	12/1	0/1	0	3/0
FA	3/1	0/0	0	0/0
Worthington	1/0	0/0	0	0/0

DANNY HAY

- **Position:** Defender
- **Born:** May 15, 1975 in Auckland (New Zealand)
- **Leeds Debut:** N/A
- **Total Leeds League Apps/Goals:** 0/0
- **Transfer:** £200,000, August 19, 1999
- **Previous Clubs:** Central United, Perth Glory
- **Club Honours:** None
- **International Honours:** Senior New Zealand international

Aware of the phenomenal success of Harry Kewell since his move from Australia, Leeds moved quickly to sign Perth Glory star Danny Hay. At 6 feet 2 inches tall and over 14 stone, the 24-year-old New Zealand international defender certainly has the physical presence to cope with the English game. Spotted on a pre-season tour of Australia in 1999, Danny was invited to join the squad's preparations and did well enough to earn himself a contract at Elland Road. With all of these impressive attributes, it's now up to the New-Zealander to force himself into the first-team frame at Elland Road. And if anyone can help him to become a top-flight defender it's David O'Leary.

Lge Games	Total mins	Goals	Star Ratings	Ave Rating
0	0	0	0	0.00

Starts	Subbed off	Subbed on	Yellow	Red
0	0	0	0	0

Cup	Games/Goals	Sub on/off	Star Ratings	Yellow/Red
All Cups	0/0	0/0	0	0/0

MARTIN HIDEN

- **Position:** Defender
- **Born:** March 11, 1973 in Stainz (Austria)
- **Leeds Debut:** February 28, 1998 v Southampton
- **Total Leeds League Apps/Goals:** 26/0
- **Transfer:** £1.3 million, February 25, 1998
- **Previous Clubs:** Rapid Vienna
- **Club Honours:** None
- **International Honours:** Senior Austria international

Competition for places in United's defence was high last season anyway, and a long-term injury hardly helped Martin Hiden's claims for a first-team place. Indeed, the Austrian defender was restricted to just one substitute appearance at the start of last season. Insufficient for an international player, Hiden decided to move to pastures new at the end of last season after never really establishing himself at Elland Road.

Lge Games	Total mins	Goals	Star Ratings	Ave Rating
1	16	0	0	0.00

Starts	Subbed off	Subbed on	Yellow	Red
0	0	1	0	0

Cup	Games/Goals	Sub on/off	Star Ratings	Yellow/Red
All Cups	0/0	0/0	0	0/0

DAVID HOPKIN

- **Position:** Midfielder
- **Born:** August 21, 1970 in Greenock
- **Leeds Debut:** August 9, 1997 v Arsenal
- **Total Leeds League Apps/Goals:** 73/6
- **Transfer:** £3.25 million, July 23, 1997
- **Previous Clubs:** Port Glasgow BC, Greenock Morton, Chelsea, Crystal Palace
- **Club Honours:** None
- **International Honours:** Senior Scotland, Scotland B international

Despite starting the season as a regular for United, David Hopkin's chances became more limited as the youngsters proved they were more than capable of making the grade. David decided to move on in the close season, with Bradford offering him the prospect of regular first-team football. Hoppy will be fondly remembered at Elland Road – he always gave 100 per cent for Leeds and the fans have always appreciated that quality, especially in their battling midfielders of the past.

Lge Games	Total mins	Goals	Star Ratings	Ave Rating
14	967	0	0	6.33

Starts	Subbed off	Subbed on	Yellow	Red
10	5	4	1	0

Cup	Games/Goals	Sub on/off	Star Ratings	Yellow/Red
UEFA	3/0	0/1	0	0/0
FA	0/0	0/0	0	0/0
Worthington	1/0	0/1	0	0/0

DARREN HUCKERBY

- **Position:** Striker
- **Born:** April 23, 1976 in Nottingham
- **Leeds Debut:** August 14, 1999 v Man. United
- **Total Leeds League Apps/Goals:** 33/2
- **Transfer:** £4 million, August 11, 1999
- **Previous Clubs:** Lincoln, Newcastle, Coventry
- **Club Honours:** None
- **International Honours:** England B, Under-21 international

Darren Huckerby arrived at United just a week after Jimmy Floyd Hasselbaink had left to join Atletico Madrid. Some fans probably saw the former Coventry forward as Hasselbaink's replacement, which must have put a lot of undue pressure on him – he's an exciting forward with phenomenal pace, but not a prolific scorer. Darren played well for Leeds last season, but rarely for the entire 90 minutes – and some supporters believe that he deserves an extended run in the starting line-up. He became United's super-sub in 1999-2000, frequently bringing a new dimension to the game with his electric pace against tiring legs. At 24, Darren still has plenty of time to improve his game, but he already gives the team a range of options so the manager can vary his tactics against different opposition.

Lge Games	Total mins	Goals	Star Ratings	Ave Rating
33	1248	2	1	6.40

Starts	Subbed off	Subbed on	Yellow	Red
9	3	24	0	0

Cup	Games/Goals	Sub on/off	Star Ratings	Yellow/Red
UEFA	9/1	8/0	0	0/0
FA	3/0	3/0	0	0/0
Worthington	1/0	1/0	0	0/0

MATTHEW **JONES**

- **Position:** Midfielder
- **Born:** September 1, 1980 in Llanelli
- **Leeds Debut:** January 23, 1999 v Portsmouth
- **Total Leeds League Apps/Goals:** 19/0
- **Transfer:** From Trainee, September 1, 1997
- **Previous Clubs:** None
- **Club Honours:** 1997 FA Youth Cup winner with Leeds
- **International Honours:** Senior, Wales B, Under-21 international

Matthew Jones committed himself to Leeds at the start of the 1999-2000 season by signing a new five-year contract. Having joined the club as a 12-year-old, Matthew has developed into an important part of the first-team squad and his versatility is a definite bonus. His potential was recognised at international level last season with his call-up to the senior Wales squad.

Lge Games	Total mins	Goals	Star Ratings	Ave Rating
11	473	0	0	6.40

Starts	Subbed off	Subbed on	Yellow	Red
5	1	6	2	0

Cup	Games/Goals	Sub on/off	Star Ratings	Yellow/Red
UEFA	5/0	2/1	0	1/0
FA	1/0	1/0	0	0/0
Worthington	1/0	1/0	0	0/0

- **Position:** Defender
- **Born:** July 9, 1974 in Drogheda
- **Leeds Debut:** December 22, 1991 v Nottingham Forest
- **Total Leeds League Apps/Goals:** 221/2
- **Transfer:** No Fee, September 24, 1991
- **Previous Clubs:** Home Farm
- **Club Honours:** 1992 Division One winner with Leeds
- **International Honours:** Senior, Under-21 Republic Of Ireland international

When he burst onto the Premiership scene in the 1993-94 season, Gary Kelly had an immediate impact, becoming one of the most promising defenders in the league. By the end of that campaign Gary had become a senior Republic Of Ireland international. However, at the start of the 1999-2000 season his long-term Leeds future was in doubt after a serious injury had kept him out for an entire year. The £4 million purchase of Charlton's promising right-back Danny Mills added to the doubts about his future, but Gary was prepared to fight for his place and is once again the first-choice right-back at Elland Road. He is comfortable on the ball, which means he can play in midfield if required, and he has also covered for Ian Harte on the left of defence when needed. The Republic of Ireland international also has lightning pace – watching Ryan Giggs against Gary Kelly is one of the greatest confrontations in the Premiership. The good news for Leeds fans is that Gary has committed himself to Elland Road for five more years, which means he'll finish his career at the top with United. Loyalty as well as everything else – Leeds through and through.

Lge Games	Total mins	Goals	Star Ratings	Ave Rating
31	2620	0	1	6.38

Starts	Subbed off	Subbed on	Yellow	Red
28	0	3	6	0

Cup	Games/Goals	Sub on/off	Star Ratings	Yellow/Red
UEFA	11/0	0/0	0	0/0
FA	3/0	0/0	0	0/0
Worthington	2/0	0/0	0	0/0

HARRY **KEWELL**

- **Position:** Midfielder/Striker
- **Born:** September 22, 1978 in Smithfield (Australia)
- **Leeds Debut:** March 30, 1996 v Middlesbrough
- **Total Leeds League Apps/Goals:** 106/21
- **Transfer:** No Fee, July 1, 1995
- **Previous Clubs:** NSW Academy
- **Club Honours:** None
- **International Honours:** Senior Australia international

Harry Kewell is the creative inspiration in this current Leeds side – his mazy runs, fancy footwork and ferocious shooting have unlocked the tightest defences in the Premiership. Harry truly came of age last season, impressing almost every time he pulled on the Leeds shirt – whether that was in Moscow, Rome or Watford. At the beginning of the 1999-2000 season, David O'Leary said that goals were the only thing missing in Harry's repertoire, but he ended the campaign on ten goals. To cap off a tremendous season he was deservedly named the Young Player Of The Year by both his fellow professionals and the Football Writers' Association. Ironically, one of the biggest problems about Harry's performances last season was that the big-spending clubs from Italy and Spain have started to take an interest in prising The Wizard of Oz away from Elland Road. However, Harry appreciates the opportunity that he was given by Leeds when he came to England and hopefully loyalty will be a deciding factor in the Australian's plans for the future.

Lge Games	Total mins	Goals	Star Ratings	Ave Rating
36	3193	10	13	7.16

Starts	Subbed off	Subbed on	Yellow	Red
36	4	0	6	0

Cup	Games/Goals	Sub on/off	Star Ratings	Yellow/Red
UEFA	12/5	0/2	4	0/1
FA	3/2	0/0	0	0/0
Worthington	2/0	0/0	1	0/0

- **Position:** Midfielder
- **Born:** November 1, 1979 in Bergen (Norway)
- **Leeds Debut:** January 23 1999 v Portsmouth
- **Total Leeds League Apps/Goals:** 0/0
- **Transfer:** No Fee, November 1, 1996
- **Previous Clubs:** Skerjgard
- **Club Honours:** None
- **International Honours:** Norway Under-16 international

Tommy Knarvik was spotted by Leeds scouts when he was playing for Norway's Under-16 team in a tournament in Dublin. Unfortunately, Norwegian football authorities were upset at losing one of their greatest talents and they refused to select him for any internationals after his transfer. Tommy has been one of the most likeable characters at Elland Road since his transfer and was named United's Young Player Of The Year in the 1998-99 season, ahead of Jonathan Woodgate and Alan Smith – which gives some indication of his potential. However, with an abundance of talented midfielders in the Leeds squad, he moved to SK Brann on a free transfer in the close season.

Lge Games	Total mins	Goals	Star Ratings	Ave Rating
0	0	0	0	0.00

Starts	Subbed off	Subbed on	Yellow	Red
0	0	0	0	0

Cup	Games/Goals	Sub on/off	Star Ratings	Yellow/Red
All Cups	0/0	0/0	0	0/0

LEE MATTHEWS

- **Position:** Striker
- **Born:** January 16, 1979 in Middlesbrough
- **Leeds Debut:** January 16, 1998 v Crystal Palace
- **Total Leeds League Apps/Goals:** 3/0
- **Transfer:** From Trainee, February 15, 1996
- **Previous Clubs:** None
- **Club Honours:** 1997 FA Youth Cup winner with Leeds
- **International Honours:** England Youth international

Unfortunately, a succession of injuries ruined Lee Matthews' chances of making a dramatic impact in the first team in the same way that many youngsters did last season for Leeds. It remains to be seen whether the 21-year-old forward, who stands at an imposing 6ft 2in, can develop into the target man that David O'Leary has been looking for. But having recovered from injury, Lee finds himself behind Harry Kewell, Michael Bridges, Darren Huckerby and Alan Smith in the competition for places. Most importantly, Mark Viduka – another big striker – has joined the club from Celtic. But this is the challenge that Lee faces. If he can impress in the reserves he knows that the manager will give him an opportunity in the first team.

Lge Games	Total mins	Goals	Star Ratings	Ave Rating
0	0	0	0	0

Starts	Subbed off	Subbed on	Yellow	Red
0	0	0	0	0

Cup	Games/Goals	Sub on/off	Star Ratings	Yellow/Red
All Cups	0/0	0/0	0	0/0

ALAN MAYBURY

- **Position:** Defender
- **Born:** August 8, 1978 in Dublin
- **Leeds Debut:** February 3, 1996 v Aston Villa
- **Total Leeds League Apps/Goals:** 13/0
- **Transfer:** August 17, 1995
- **Previous Clubs:** St Kevins BC, Reading (on loan)
- **Club Honours:** 1997 FA Youth Cup winner with Leeds
- **International Honours:** Republic Of Ireland (squad)

Alan Maybury was captain of the Leeds side that won the FA Youth Cup in 1997, and before last season he was pushing Gary Kelly for the right-back slot. But when Kelly picked up his long-term injury, Alan was suffering from shin splints. Unfortunately, by the time he was ready to return, Kelly had also recovered from his injury and Leeds had added Danny Mills to the squad. While Alan has struggled since his injury, he'll want to work get his head down now and work hard on his fitness so the management at Leeds can't ignore him.

Lge Games	Total mins	Goals	Star Ratings	Ave Rating
0	0	0	0	0.00

Starts	Subbed off	Subbed on	Yellow	Red
0	0	0	0	0

Cup	Games/Goals	Sub on/off	Star Ratings	Yellow/Red
All Cups	0/0	0/0	0	0/0

- **Position:** Goalkeeper
- **Born:** August 11, 1966 in St Austell
- **Leeds Debut:** August 17, 1996 v Derby
- **Total Leeds League Apps/Goals:** 146/0
- **Transfer:** £2.5 million, July 24, 1996
- **Previous Clubs:** Bristol Rovers, Crystal Palace
- **Club Honours:** 1994 Division One winner with Crystal Palace
- **International Honours:** Senior England, Under-21 international

What a season Nigel Martyn had last year. If there was a vote of the public to decide England's number one 'keeper, he'd surely be the clear winner. In a team packed with young, often inexperienced players, Nigel is a reassuring presence in the Leeds goal. An excellent all-round goalkeeper, he is most renowned for his shot-stopping, which saved Leeds on many occasions last season. But he's not just a big-game performer, Nigel is a consistent goalkeeper who earned Leeds as many points as the strikers last season. One of his finest displays was in the away leg of the UEFA Cup fourth round, when he performed heroically to keep Leeds in the tie against Roma. The talented Italian side put Leeds under constant pressure, and the defence was repeatedly opened up, but Roma just couldn't get past the Leeds No. 1 who put in a memorable performance – the best 'keeper in the Premiership bar none.

Lge Games	Total mins	Goals	Star Ratings	Ave Rating
38	3420	0	2	6.60

Starts	Subbed off	Subbed on	Yellow	Red
38	0	0	2	0

Cup	Game/Goals	Sub on/off	Star Ratings	Yellow/Red
UEFA	12/0	0/0	1	0/0
FA	3/0	0/0	0	0/0
Worthington	2/0	0/0	0	0/0

STEPHEN McPHAIL

- **Position:** Midfield
- **Born:** December 9, 1979 in London
- **Leeds Debut:** February 7, 1998 v Leicester
- **Total Leeds League Apps/Goals:** 45/2
- **Transfer:** From Trainee, December 9, 1996
- **Previous Clubs:** None
- **Club Honours:** 1997 FA Youth Cup winner with Leeds
- **International Honours:** Senior, Under-21 Republic Of Ireland international

They've been talking about Stephen McPhail at Elland Road for a long time now. He started last season with an injury but by the end he'd become a first-team regular. Coming through the ranks as a gifted left-footed midfielder with Irish roots, he has been compared with Arsenal great Liam Brady, which just shows how highly he is rated. Leeds fans will expect even bigger things from the Irishman this season and will wonder if he can claim a permanent place in a competitive midfield.

Lge Games	Total mins	Goals	Star Ratings	Ave Rating
23	2063	2	3	6.58

Starts	Subbed off	Subbed on	Yellow	Red
23	3	1	0	0

Cup	Games/Goals	Sub on/off	Star Ratings	Yellow/Red
UEFA	9/0	0/3	0	0/0
FA	3/0	0/0	1	0/0
Worthington	2/0	1/0	0	0/0

DANNY MILLS

- **Position:** Defender
- **Born:** May 18, 1977 in Norwich
- **Leeds Debut:** August 7, 1999 v Derby County
- **Total Leeds League Apps/Goals:** 17/1
- **Transfer:** £4 million, June 15, 1999
- **Previous Clubs:** Charlton Athletic
- **Club Honours:** None
- **International Honours:** England Under-21, Under-18, Under-16 international

Leeds were after full-back Danny Mills for a long time (almost six months) before he finally signed on the dotted line in June 1999 for £4 million. Danny played well at the beginning of the season but Gary Kelly's return to form after injury meant he had to watch from the sidelines for much of 1999-2000. But Mills will continue to get opportunities at Leeds – his versatility and wholehearted commitment mean he'll remain an important part of the United squad for some time to come. Danny has played at centre-back when the team played with a back five, which was another reason why David O'Leary was delighted to secure his signature with several top clubs also interested. His finest moment of the season was scoring a late winner against Sunderland back in August, and Danny will be looking for more of the same this season. The important thing is that United have two quality players battling for the right-back position. Other Premiership managers will be envious of that kind of talent as Leeds go for glory again this time around.

Lge Games	Total mins	Goals	Star Ratings	Ave Rating
17	1463	1	1	6.47

Starts	Subbed off	Subbed on	Yellow	Red
16	1	1	5	0

Cup	Games/Goals	Sub on/off	Star Ratings	Yellow/Red
UEFA	2/0	0/0	0	0/0
FA	1/0	1/0	0	0/0
Worthington	1/1	0/0	0	0/0

ROBERT MOLENAAR

- **Position:** Defender
- **Born:** February 27, 1969 in Zaandam (Holland)
- **Leeds Debut:** January 22, 1997 v Leicester
- **Total Leeds League Apps/Goals:** 51/5
- **Transfer:** £1 million, January 11, 1997
- **Previous Clubs:** FC Volendam
- **Club Honours:** None
- **International Honours:** None

Robert Molenaar was a regular fixture in the Leeds defence until he suffered a cruciate knee injury in a clash with Arsenal in December 1998. Robert was making a good recovery until he ruptured the same knee in pre-season training last year. Since then the Dutchman hasn't played for Leeds, but he has signed a one-year extension to his contract, so he's obviously a valued member of David O'Leary's squad. Robert spent the end of 1999-2000 rebuilding his match fitness in the reserves and will now be pushing for a return to first-team action.

Lge Games	Total mins	Goals	Star Ratings	Ave Rating
0	0	0	0	0

Starts	Subbed off	Subbed on	Yellow	Red
0	0	0	0	0

Cup	Games/Goals	Sub on/off	Star Ratings	Yellow/Red
All Cups	0/0	0/0	0	0/0

LUCAS RADEBE

- **Position:** Defender
- **Born:** April 12, 1969, in Johannesburg (South Africa)
- **Leeds Debut:** September 7, 1994 v Sheff. Wed.
- **Total Leeds League Apps/Goals:** 144/0
- **Transfer:** £250,000, September 5, 1994
- **Previous Clubs:** Kaiser Chiefs
- **Club Honours:** None
- **International Honours:** Senior South Africa international

Lucas Radebe is one of the best defenders to wear the Leeds colours since the glory days of the '70s. Signed by Howard Wilkinson in 1994 for the bargain price of £250,000, there are many attributes to the skipper's game. It's not just big Lucas' enormous physical presence or his superb tackling that makes him so exceptional – his superb positioning means he's rarely caught out. Last season was another vintage campaign for the Leeds captain, who turned in some magnificent displays for The Whites – notably in their tough European games away from home, when his marshalling of the Leeds back line was outstanding. Another experienced player in an otherwise young team, Lucas could prove to be the difference between Leeds being exciting also-rans and major trophy winners in the next few seasons. Now 31, the skipper still has a good few years left at the top and he has already pledged his future to United after a number of approaches from abroad. Another loyal member of David O'Leary's squad, Lucas wants to repay the club for showing faith in him when he arrived at Leeds.

Lge Games	Total mins	Goals	Star Ratings	Ave Rating
31	2696	0	3	6.87

Starts	Subbed off	Subbed on	Yellow	Red
31	2	0	2	0

Cup	Games/Goals	Sub on/off	Star Ratings	Yellow/Red
UEFA	11/2	0/0	0	2/0
FA	2/0	0/0	0	0/0
Worthington	2/0	0/0	0	0/1

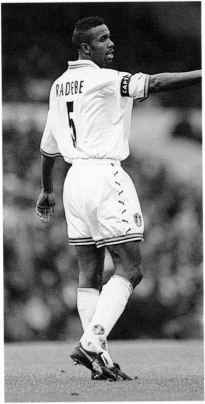

DAVID ROBERTSON

- **Position:** Defender
- **Born:** October 17, 1968 in Aberdeen
- **Leeds Debut:** August 9, 1997 v Arsenal
- **Total Leeds League Apps/Goals:** 26/0
- **Transfer:** £500,000, May 12, 1997
- **Previous Clubs:** Aberdeen, Rangers
- **Club Honours:** Scottish Premier League winner with Aberdeen (1989, 1990, 1991) and Rangers (1992, 1993, 1994, 1995, 1996, 1997); Scottish Cup winner with Aberdeen (1990) and Rangers (1992, 1993, 1996); Scottish League Cup winner with Aberdeen (1990) and Rangers (1993, 1994, 1997)
- **International Honours:** Senior, Scotland B, Under-21 Scotland international

It's been a frustrating time for David Robertson since joining Leeds from Rangers in 1997. After enjoying great success in Scotland, he took time to settle at Elland Road. David found his feet, but after picking up an injury, Ian Harte stepped in and made the left-back position his own. He didn't start any games for Leeds last season and turned down a loan move.

Lge Games	Total mins	Goals	Star Ratings	Ave Rating
0	0	0	0	0

Starts	Subbed off	Subbed on	Yellow	Red
0	0	0	0	0

Cup	Games/Goals	Sub on/off	Star Ratings	Yellow/Red
All Cups	0/0	0/0	0	0/0

PAUL ROBINSON

- **Position:** Goalkeeper
- **Born:** October 15, 1979 in Beverley
- **Leeds Debut:** October 25, 1998 v Chelsea
- **Total Leeds League Apps/Goals:** 5/0
- **Transfer:** From Trainee, May 31, 1997
- **Previous Clubs:** None
- **Club Honours:** 1997 FA Youth Cup winner with Leeds
- **International Honours:** England Under-21, Under-18 international

Paul Robinson has emerged as Elland Road's second-choice 'keeper after long-term understudy Mark Beeney was forced to retire through injury. Despite limited chances in the first team, Paul has always impressed when he has been called upon. Nigel Martyn was an ever present last season as Paul had to look on from the sidelines, but the 1997 FA Youth Cup winner will surely get his chance to impress if he is patient.

Lge Games	Total mins	Goals	Star Ratings	Ave Rating
0	0	0	0	0

Starts	Subbed off	Subbed on	Yellow	Red
0	0	0	0	0

Cup	Games/Goals	Sub on/off	Star Ratings	Yellow/Red
All Cups	0/0	0/0	0	0/0

ALAN SMITH

- **Position:** Striker
- **Born:** October 28, 1980 in Rothwell
- **Leeds Debut:** November 14, 1998 v Liverpool
- **Total Leeds League Apps/Goals:** 48/11
- **Transfer:** From Trainee, October 1997
- **Previous Clubs:** None
- **Club Honours:** 1997 FA Youth Cup winner with Leeds
- **International Honours:** England Under-21, Youth international

Alan Smith ended 1998-99 as the preferred strike partner of Jimmy Floyd Hasselbaink and signed a new five-year deal to stay at Elland Road – it was a dramatic rise to fame. However, last season was frustrating for Smithy – the competition for places has increased now in the Leeds squad and Alan faces a battle for his place with the signing of Mark Viduka, the new role that Harry Kewell adopts alongside Michael Bridges, and the presence of fellow striker Darren Huckerby. But Alan is up for the challenge and he was delighted to get the support of his manager before the start of the new 2000-2001 season. It was David O'Leary who gave Alan his chance in the Leeds first team – and the former trainee repaid this faith by scoring on his debut against Liverpool in November 1998. The striker now wants to repay the club and realises this is an exciting time to be a part of the revolution at Elland Road. That is why, despite the speculation, Alan has pledged his future to Leeds, who are closer to silverware than the clubs he was linked with.

Lge Games	Total mins	Goals	Star Ratings	Ave Rating
26	1738	4	0	6.12

Starts	Subbed off	Subbed on	Yellow	Red
20	11	6	6	1

Cup	Games/Goals	Sub on/off	Star Ratings	Yellow/Red
UEFA	8/1	5/1	0	2/0
FA	3/1	1/2	0	2/0
Worthington	1/0	0	0	1/0

JASON WILCOX

- **Position:** Midfielder
- **Born:** July 15, 1971 in Bolton
- **Leeds Debut:** December 19, 1999 v Chelsea
- **Total Leeds League Apps/Goals:** 20/3
- **Transfer:** £3 million, December 17, 1999
- **Previous Clubs:** Blackburn Rovers
- **Club Honours:** 1995 Premier League winner with Blackburn
- **International Honours:** Senior England international

When Jason Wilcox moved to Elland Road, Blackburn Rovers received £3 million to spend on their squad and Leeds got a talented, experienced left-sided player. Jason soon earned himself a recall to the England squad after rediscovering his form in the Premiership. His ability on the left allowed David O'Leary to push Harry Kewell forward to play as a striker last season, with great results. Jason is also a model professional and sets a fine example to the young members of the squad.

Lge Games	Total mins	Goals	Star Ratings	Ave Rating
20	1422	3	0	6.76

Starts	Subbed off	Subbed on	Yellow	Red
15	3	5	1	0

Cup	Games/Goals	Sub on/off	Star Ratings	Yellow/Red
UEFA	3/1	1/0	1	1/0
FA	2/0	0/0	0	1/0
Worthington	0/0	0/0	0	0/0

JONATHAN WOODGATE

- **Position:** Defender
- **Born:** January 22, 1980 in Middlesbrough
- **Leeds Debut:** October 17, 1998 v Nottingham Forest
- **Total Leeds League Apps/Goals:** 59/3
- **Transfer:** From Trainee August 1, 1998
- **Previous Clubs:** None
- **Club Honours:** None
- **International Honours:** Senior England, Under-21, Under-18 international

Even in United's squad of youngsters, it's hard to believe that Jonathan Woodgate is still only 20-years-old. Jonathan has already got a senior England cap and is a permanent fixture in the centre of the Leeds rearguard alongside Lucas Radebe. Singled out by George Graham as the best of a great crop of Leeds youngsters, it wasn't until David O'Leary's second game in charge at Elland Road that he got his chance. Since then Jonathan has never looked back. Last season was something of a mixed bag for the defender though. He started the season in truly superb form before problems off the field affected his performances. The Leeds faithful will hope that he is back to his best this season as the team challenge for major honours. Woody is one of a small crop of English central defenders who is comfortable on the ball and more than capable of bringing it out of defence. Like his captain at Leeds, Lucas Radebe, the towering centre-back reads the game superbly and his powers of recovery are superb – which are two important qualities for a central defender. At the age of 20 Woody will only get better for both Leeds and England – and what a prospect that is.

Lge Games	Total mins	Goals	Star Ratings	Ave Rating
34	2816	1	1	6.73

Starts	Subbed off	Subbed on	Yellow	Red
2816	3	2	0	0

Cup	Games/Goals	Sub on/off	Star Ratings	Yellow/Red
UEFA	10/0	0/0	0	1/0
FA	3/0	0/0	0	0/0
Worthington	2/0	0/0	0	0/0

TRANSFER ROUND-UP

WHEN LEEDS CHAIRMAN PETER RIDSDALE predicted that Olivier Dacourt – at £8 million – would not be the club's record signing by the beginning of the new season, the press linked Leeds with a host of players. At the top of the list was a big-name striker, and after several months of speculation and work permit doubts, The Whites unveiled Celtic's prolific star Mark Viduka for £6 million. Leeds supporters were thrilled to see David O'Leary add to his young squad with two such accomplished players.

Dominic Matteo should have been the third major signing of the summer, but the versatile Liverpool defender failed a medical at Elland Road. His £4 million transfer from Anfield still looks likely, but reports linking Leeds with West Ham defender Rio Ferdinand seem wide of the mark. David O'Leary now wants his current side to stay together for a number of years so they can challenge Manchester United for the title.

Three members of the Leeds squad left the club during the close season. David Hopkin had limited chances after the emergence of younger players in midfield and moved to Bradford for £2.5 million. Alf-Inge Haaland deputised in both defence and midfield last season but moved to Manchester City for £2.8 million after realising he could spend most of the new season on the Leeds bench. Martin Hiden was a permanent fixture for The Whites until he suffered a serious injury in November 1998. The Austrian defender moved home in the summer to join SV Salzburg for £500,000. All three players left Leeds with the club wishing them well for the future.

MARK **VIDUKA**

- **Position:** Striker
- **Born:** October 9, 1975 in Melbourne, Australia
- **Leeds Debut:** August 9, 2000 v 1860 Munich
- **Transfer:** £6 million, July 21, 2000
- **Previous Clubs:** Croatia Zagreb, Celtic
- **Club Honours:** 2000 Scottish League Cup winner with Celtic
- **International Honours:** Senior Australia international

Mark Viduka first arrived on British shores to play for Celtic after signing from Croatia Zagreb in November 1998. Mark had impressed the Glasgow club after playing against them in the 1998 Champions League – and beating The Bhoys at home and in Scotland. But the striker had a bad start to his Celtic career after returning home to Australia just days after arriving at the club. Mark was suffering from a stress-related illness and Celtic withheld some of the transfer fee until he returned to the club after a period of recuperation.

When he arrived back in Scotland he made a sensational impact. From his very first game at Parkhead he showed the fans what a superb all-round player he is. Mark is tall, strong and athletic, so defenders always know they've got a game on their hands when they face him. Most importantly, he scores goals for fun. His average of scoring a goal every game in the Scottish Premier League is hugely impressive. Some observers say it's easier to score in Scotland's top-flight than in the Premiership, but David O'Leary has shown himself to be a shrewd judge of players and every purchase he has made so far has been carefully planned.

In excelling for Celtic last season, Mark showed far more than just the predatory instincts of a natural goalscorer. With his physique and ability, he should be able to hold the ball up well and bring some of United's other attacking players into play. Jimmy Floyd Hasselbaink may have been a prolific striker during his time with Leeds, but the Dutchman didn't gain a reputation at Elland Road for being a team player.

If Mark Viduka turns out to be the striker David O'Leary has been chasing for so long, Leeds fans can expect to see their side mount a serious and sustained challenge for the Premiership title this season. The big Australian striker could even form an awesome attacking trio with Harry Kewell and Michael Bridges. Imagine facing those three on a Saturday afternoon – Premiership defences will be dreading it.

OLIVIER **DACOURT**

- **Position:** Midfielder
- **Born:** September 29, 1974 in Paris
- **Leeds Debut:** August 9, 2000 v 1860 Munich
- **Transfer:** £7.2 million, May 15, 2000
- **Previous Clubs:** Lens, Everton, Strasbourg, Aulnay sous Bois
- **Club Honours:** None
- **International Honours:** None

Tough-tackling, strong and determined. Sound familiar? With the long-term injury to David Batty, Leeds broke their transfer record to secure the services of Olivier Dacourt from Lens for £7.2 million. A similar player to Batty, Olivier boasts a natural attacking instinct and is an excellent passer of the ball. David O'Leary says Leeds missed the experience of Batty in midfield last season so Olivier should help to solve this problem.

The Frenchman has experience of Premiership football and impressed during his time at Goodison Park in the 1998-99 season. Many foreign stars represent a risk to managers because there are doubts about whether they will adapt to the demands of the Premiership. But Olivier proved he was more than capable of settling in on Merseyside and was probably Everton's best player before leaving the club after one season.

The combative midfielder needs to avoid the disciplinary problems which marred his previous spell in England. In the 1998-99 season at Everton he received 13 bookings and one red card – a record that compares with his close friend and compatriot Patrick Vieira. However, Olivier insists that he has learned to deal with his temperament, which must be a relief to David O'Leary. So if anyone thinks the Leeds midfield will become a shadow of its former combative self in the absence of David Batty, they should think again. Olivier Dacourt looks likely to make a very distinctive mark on the Premiership this season for United – and for all the right reasons.

THE SQUAD

1. Nigel **Martyn**
2. Gary **Kelly**
3. Ian **Harte**
4. Olivier **Dacourt**
5. Lucas **Radebe**
6. Jonathan **Woodgate**
7.
8. Michael **Bridges**
9. Mark **Viduka**
10. Harry **Kewell**
11. Lee **Bowyer**
12. Darren **Huckerby**
13. Paul **Robinson**
14. Stephen **McPhail**
15.
16. Jason **Wilcox**
17. Alan **Smith**
18. Danny **Mills**
19. Eirik **Bakke**
20. Matthew **Jones**
21.
22. Michael **Duberry**
23. David **Batty**
24. Danny **Hay**
25.
26. Danny **Milosevic**
27. Alan **Maybury**
28. Jamie **McMaster**
29. Kevin **Evans**
30. Robert **Molenaar**
31. Gareth **Evans**
32. Simon **Watson**
33. Wesley **Boyle**
34. Kevin **Dixon**
35. Lee **Matthews**
36. Warren **Feeney**
37. Damien **Lynch**
38. Tony **Hackworth**
39. Alan **Martin**
40. Alan **Cawley**
41. Jason **Lanns**
42. Tony **Lennon**
43. Harpal **Singh**

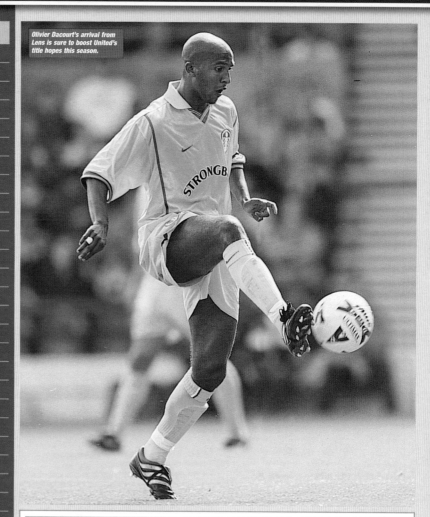

Olivier Dacourt's arrival from Lens is sure to boost United's title hopes this season.

LEEDS UNITED FIXTURES

Aug. 19	**Everton**	H	Dec. 26	Newcastle United	A
Aug. 23	Aston Villa	A	Dec. 30	Everton	A
Aug. 26	Middlesbrough	A	Jan. 1	**Middlesbrough**	H
Sept. 5	**Manchester City**	H	Jan. 13	Manchester City	A
Sept. 9	Coventry City	A	Jan. 20	**Newcastle United**	H
Sept. 16	**Ipswich Town**	H	Jan. 30	**Coventry City**	H
Sept. 23	Derby County	A	Feb. 3	Ipswich Town	A
Sept. 30	**Tottenham Hotspur**	H	Feb. 10	**Derby County**	H
Oct. 14	**Charlton Athletic**	H	Feb. 24	Tottenham Hotspur	A
Oct. 21	Manchester United	A	Mar. 3	**Manchester United**	H
Oct. 29	Bradford City	A	Mar. 17	Charlton Athletic	A
Nov. 4	**Liverpool**	H	Mar. 31	Sunderland	A
Nov. 12	Chelsea	A	Apr. 7	**Southampton**	H
Nov. 18	**West Ham United**	H	Apr. 14	Liverpool	A
Nov. 26	**Arsenal**	H	Apr. 17	**Bradford City**	H
Dec. 2	Leicester City	A	Apr. 21	West Ham United	A
Dec. 9	Southampton	A	Apr. 28	**Chelsea**	H
Dec. 16	**Sunderland**	H	May 5	Arsenal	A
Dec. 23	**Aston Villa**	H	May 19	**Leicester City**	H